HOW DID YOU GET STARTED, VOLUME I:

Inspiring Stories of Successful Business Professionals

Felicia J. Slattery

ISBN 13 TP: 978-0-9822525-0-5
ISBN 13 eBook: 978-0-9822525-1-2

Library of Congress Control Number: 2018959592

ParkHill Press
1059 N. Cedar Bluff Road, Suite 177
Knoxville, Tennessee 37923
United States

Contact the Editor: http://FeliciaSlattery.com/contact

Ordering Information:
Quantity sales. Special discounts are available on quantity purchases by corporations, associations, and others. For details, contact the Editor at the address above.

For Worldwide Distribution, Printed in the U.S.A.

DEDICATION

To every person with a dream of doing work you love to do, may you be inspired to move in that direction more every day.

To all the members of Networking Today International in Knoxville and beyond, keep meeting and doing great things to support each other and helping each other's businesses succeed.

TABLE OF CONTENTS

FOREWORD

By: Rich DeForest

As the CEO and founder of Networking Today International, I thank you for your interest in reading this book, "How Did You Get Started." I can tell you I am absolutely blessed to be a part of this book as well as all the members of Networking Today International who are involved in writing chapters in this book, some of whom have been with Networking Today from the very start of it all back in 2013 in that little coffeehouse in the Karns area in Knoxville, Tennessee. We even have some newer members participating, which shows the tremendous growth and strength of our networking efforts over the years.

It is my intention and my hope every word of this book does nothing but encourage you and inspire you to take the next step in your journey of entrepreneurship and business success. May every sentence you read, in every chapter you explore, including my own, inspire you to either get started or keep going. The journey of entrepreneurship offers freedom for you, and for your family and can be passed on generation after generation. I hope that is exactly the outcome after you finish each chapter of this book. Thanks again - and enjoy!

- Rich DeForest, CEO and Founder,
Networking Today International

INTRODUCTION

By: Felicia Slattery

The beginning.

Beginnings are what "How Did You Get Started" is all about, but it's so much more than that.

Sure, the question, "How Did You Get Started?" is ideal for the beginning of a new business relationship and what to say when you meet someone new, as I've written about in my Amazon #1 best-selling book, "Kill the Elevator Speech." With that one simple question, you can quickly cut through the weird awkwardness that so many people feel when networking or meeting someone new for the first time using those five simple little words. In fact, I teach those words: "How Did You Get Started" to every audience I speak to on stages around the world because they are so important, helpful, and powerful for making a true connection with another human being in those first moments of meeting each other.

Yet "How Did You Get Started" goes even deeper than that.

It's about connecting with other people, hearing their stories to find common ground, learning from their mistakes, and celebrating their triumphs.

It's about giving others hope that there are an unlimited number of ways to reach success, and, yes, even your path can lead there.

It's about encouraging people to investigate something new, look at where they've been, and discover appreciation for their own journey up until now, no matter what that's looked like and to know they CAN go on to create the life and business of their dreams.

Putting together this first "How Did You Get Started" book has been an honor and a privilege. Given that it is the first book in the series, I suppose answering how the "How Did You Get Started" book should be told right about now.

How This Book Got Started

On March 1, 2018, I attended a Knoxville, Tennessee Chamber of Commerce event called "Schmoozapalooza" (fun name, right?!). While walking the floor, going from vendor table to vendor table, I met Allen McMichael of Fostering Hope, Tennessee (you can read his story in Chapter 5), who told me about a networking group called Networking Today International (NTi). After a few minutes, he introduced me to the founder of Networking Today, Rich DeForest (the author of this book's Foreword with his story in Chapter 0). We chatted a bit, but as you can imagine, it was a busy event, so they invited me to attend an upcoming NTi meeting and I moved along.

About two weeks later I attended my first Networking Today International meeting, and I was hooked. You see, when I started my business in 2006 in Chicagoland, I attended a weekly networking meeting called Leading the Way in Naperville, Illinois and continued for nine years, before my husband and I relocated our family to Knoxville. I love those people and I miss them. That meeting was (and still is) on Thursday mornings, and it may sound silly, but when I learned my local Networking Today International meeting was also on Thursday mornings, at the perfect time for my schedule, I felt like it was a wink from God saying, "This is the group for you to join." I love listening to the promptings of the Holy Spirit in my soul, because joining that group has changed my life and launched this new path for me.

Now, before going on, I should tell you, most of my business does not come from what you might consider a "typical" local business owner who might be attending a networking meeting. With tens of thousands of people from 81 countries having subscribed to my online community and free tools, most of my living comes from businesses and people across the country and around the world. For me to be able to speak on stages, work with clients, write books, and do all the various tasks that come with a professional speaking business, I need an internet connection and an airport, and little else to run my business. My clients are coaches, consultants, speakers, and authors themselves, or those who want to be. They are people who want to learn effective communication skills for their businesses, and how to use public speaking as a way to grow their businesses. Sometimes I meet them as I network locally (like Keith

Galloway, author of Chapter 12), but generally, I like to attend networking meetings near my home for three reasons:

I love meeting business people and hearing their stories (and getting out of the house and away from the computer for my own piece of mind!).

I need local products and services myself and for my family and I like to work with people I know and trust, who I see on a regular basis.

I enjoy watching people present and speak about their businesses, which allows me to be "in the trenches" seeing what works so I can share it with my clients and online communities (email subscribers, social media friends, and on my blog, too).

Within a few weeks of me joining NTi, Rich DeForest approached me with an idea for his own book, and as we talked, I realized there would be a way we could accomplish several goals at once: he could become an author (and now he is!), we could provide an opportunity for members of NTi to also become authors without having to write and publish a whole book, and I could provide value to the wonderful, smart, successful members of NTi using the book writing, publishing, and marketing skills I've gained myself over the years. It was a true win-win-win situation, which is the only way I like to work.

You're holding the result in your hands right now and I couldn't be prouder of the hard work this group of authors has put in to bring you their amazing stories.

Did You Say Volume 1?

You may have noticed on the cover; this book is Volume 1. I'm thrilled Rich DeForest agreed to have this first collection of stories come exclusively from members of Networking Today International. But that "Volume 1" on the cover means you can expect to see more interesting, informative, and inspiring stories from people all over the world, doing all kinds of work. I see it as a sort of "Chicken Soup for the Soul®" series, but all about how people got started doing the work they love to do. If you've got a story to tell that led to your success or if you lead a fabulous group of people with stories to tell, I might love to feature you and yours in an upcoming edition. My contact info is at the end of this introduction.

So Why Chapter 0?

It's unusual to have a "Chapter 0" in a book, but there's a specific reason why I created this book with it. Rich DeForest's story of how Networking Today International came into existence is Chapter 0 because every one of the authors in this book is a member of Networking Today International, and from Knoxville, Tennessee. Networking Today in Knoxville is the "ground zero" of sorts - it's the place all these people have met, all these people have been a part of, and a place all these people find others to do business with and support. As the founder of NTi, Rich's story and vision of an organization he treats like family, came before the beginning of anything else... and so I will leave you to begin with the story of how Networking Today

International got started, by its founder, and my friend, Rich DeForest.

Warmly,
Felicia J. Slattery, M.A., M.Ad.Ed.

#1 Best-Selling Author, Speaker, Speech Coach, and Communication Consultant
http://FeliciaSlattery.com

http://HowDidYouGetStartedShow.com
(the podcast and live radio show)

I'm on social media sites as "@FeliciaSlattery" including LinkedIn, Twitter, Facebook, YouTube, Pinterest, Instagram, Quora... you name it!

Contact me at: http://FeliciaSlattery.com/contact

CHAPTER 0

Networking Today, Yesterday, and Tomorrow with Positive Consequences

By: Rich DeForest

My whole purpose in being a part of a book that would compile a variety of authors who would share their "How Did You Get Started" story is to encourage and inspire you, the reader, to never give up on your dream; you know, that dream of grandeur you had when you were just a kid. The truth is, we've all got a story. One day, it's my hope that the world is reading yours, but your story will never be known if you quit too early. Never, I repeat, never quit.

One thing is for sure, if you would have asked me just three to five years ago if I would be CEO of the fastest-growing business referral networking organization in the country, I would have laughed. Networking Today International's (NTi) success was unintentional. Of course, starting NTi was quite intentional, but the reason I started NTi was to give my web development company, fanplicity, more visibility and exposure – I needed more referrals at fanplicity or the company was going to die. Knowing I needed more visibility and exposure, I was motivated to build a network of other business professionals that could refer fanplicity to any and all of their contacts who needed our products and services. It's the sole reason I started NTi. I had a need, and with a lack of solutions in the market, I created something that would meet my need. For me it was simple supply and demand economics.

Unintentional Consequences of Intentional Actions

As you read my chapter, I want you to keep this one phrase in your mind, "the unintentional consequences of intentional actions." By the end of this chapter, I hope you'll begin to understand the importance of taking action; better said, DO SOMETHING! Newton's first Law of Motion says that "an object either remains at rest or continues to move at a constant velocity, unless acted upon by a force" Karma refers to this as the Law of Cause and Effect. The Bible calls it sowing and reaping. Regardless of what you call it, it is a universal law that something, good or not-so-good will come from you doing something – any something.

I will continue sharing my story, but let me ask you to think about something: can you get interest from an account with no money in it? Can you get heat from a fireplace with no wood first being set on fire in it? Can you win the lottery without first buying a ticket? The answer to each of these questions is exactly the same, and of course, to state the obvious, the answer is no. I can hear you saying, "Thank you Captain Obvious!" Okay, but here's what I've learned: when you do something, take some sort of action, the law of motion demands that the universe find a way to react. If you sow something good, something good must come back to you. If you invest a lot of hours in doing nothing, you'll get a lot of nothing in return. You see? When you do something, anything, something must happen even if you don't know what it will be.

Early Days Meeting in the Loft of a Coffee Shop

Now then, with that as the backdrop, let me tell you "HOW" I got started. In July of 2013, I asked three friends to join me in the loft of a coffee shop on the northwest side of Knoxville, Tennessee. I wanted to tell them about this great idea I had to launch a new business networking meeting that would increase exposure to every participating company, and maybe even some that didn't participate. My three friends agreed to meet. At the time, I barely had a rough outline of how our meeting would differentiate itself from any other networking meeting, but we knew enough to get started. My goal was simple: I needed to do something to help myself, my business, and others and their businesses. So, we all agreed to start meeting every Thursday from 9:00 to 10:30 a.m. Additionally, we all agreed to spread the word to our existing networks. From there, with no literature, no website, no brand, no logo, no business plan, no staff, and no resources Networking Today International was launched.

Within just a few months, we'd grown from me plus three to six, then to 12, then, what felt like overnight, we had standing room only in that coffee house loft, with 40-plus people in attendance each week. What followed surprised me even more; a fellow networker, Todd Olson, approached me asking to start a second meeting, then Brian Williams started a third, and before I knew it, we had eight meetings across and throughout the greater Knoxville area – it was amazing!

However, by the end of 2016, NTi was demanding more time than I could afford to give it; a change was needed. About a year earlier, we had created a membership payment method to generate revenue; however, it proved to be inadequate to support the growing demands of a professionally-organized referral meeting. My good friend and part-time business coach, Coley Pardue from Anchor Services, referred to me as "the man in the dark blue suit!" I was afraid to ask what that meant, but I had to know. Coley said, "The man of the dark blue suit, he pisses in his pants. It gives him a warm feeling, and no one notices!" I replied saying, "yes, but there's one thing you left out... after only a few short minutes, he feels uncomfortably cold, wet, and he smells bad!" At that moment I determined to close seven of the meetings leaving only my own to run and manage. I remember agonizing over the ultimate demise of their networking meeting, knowing it would negatively impact their members. Nonetheless, despite my heartbreak and disappointment, my responsibility was to my staff at fanplicity and my family at home, so I proceeded to meet with each NTi Meeting Leader individually, informing them of my intention to close their meetings.

Time to Shut Down ... Or ... Maybe Not!

What happened next would change my life for the better. Every single meeting leader asked to keep going; they concurred that if we closed, it would have a serious negative impact on every person involved. They fought back saying they and their members wanted to be a part of something bigger than just a single meeting. They said that we had created something special in NTi that was different than every other meeting; they said, there must be a way to keep going! To say I was surprised would be a serious understatement! Happy, but confused and uncertain about the future, we persisted. In January of 2017, I asked each of the Meeting Leaders to help raise funds for the financial needs of the company. In all, we raised only $500, which was nowhere near enough to support our young and growing organization.

Then, in February 2017, during a meeting leader team meeting, I informed all the meeting leaders we would begin charging a customary membership fee. I shared how I had taken several weeks to survey several members from a variety of different types of businesses asking them how many sales they would need to cover a $25 per month or $250 annual membership... not one said more than three. That's right! Three sales or less would cover the cost of their annual membership to NTi. So, now I was about to announce the cost of membership, believing it to be a reasonable price for everyone.

Next came my mind-blowing revelation. Somewhere around the 15th of February, during my meeting, I announced that we would begin charging for membership the very next week, and if members wanted to stay a part of NTi, they would need to begin paying monthly or annually. Ready to have your mind blown? Members started walking up to me and other meeting leadership handing us checks for membership. That's right, you read that right, members were handing us membership checks, some for a full year in advance! And, did I mention that it was on the very same day I announced it!?! I drove to my home office dazed and confused at what had just happened – my mind had been blown and I was in shock! I didn't know exactly what to expect when we announced we were going to start charging people for what had always been free or close to it, but in the back of my mind I was worried people would rebel, and membership might drop significantly. Yet, it was at that moment I realized and understood, perhaps for the first time in my entire life, that people have no problem paying for something they see value in. The problem wasn't that the *membership* didn't see the value of NTi, it was that *I* didn't see the value of membership. BOOM! (That was the sound of my mind blowing.) You could have knocked me over with a feather! The next week, Sharon Cawood, a long-time member and good friend from N2 Publishing, said something to me I will never forget as long as I live. She said, "Now you can grow NTi!" I understood, again, for the first time ever, that if we had no means of generating revenue, we would have no means to grow or even a reason to do so – Sharon was so incredibly correct!

Expanding Beyond the Mother Ship and Outside Knoxville

In March of 2017, just one month later, I reached out to a friend I'd become close to while we worked together when fanplicity had Jet's Pizza as a customer, Marketing and Accounting Manager, MaryAnn Palise. Now a successful realtor in Nashville, Tennessee, Mary Ann agreed to be the first NTi meeting outside of Knoxville. We had to test our ability to maintain our amazing culture beyond the reach of the Mother Ship, so to speak. MaryAnn exceeded every expectation by not only having a 35-plus member meeting herself in Brentwood, but she would help NTi add an additional five meeting locations across the Nashville area. Again, at the risk of being redundant, my mind was blown one more time.

By March 2018, NTi had grown to more than 40 meeting locations expanding to Springfield, Missouri with Kristina Parry, Missy Martin, and Mark Williams leading the charge. Then onto St. Louis, Missouri with Tara Peterson at the helm there, now boasting a wildly successful 50-plus member meeting location. At the time of this writing Tara has helped develop St. Louis to 11 NTi meeting locations along with Deanna and Chris Ley. Next, with Rockford Stites from Primerica leading the charge, we've grown to six meeting locations throughout Indianapolis, Indiana. We are humbled and happy to work with such an amazing team of leaders!

What's next for NTi? The world! We want to improve business referral networking in every city around the world and beyond! We want to share our vision for a better quality of networking by focusing on establishing new and strengthening existing relationships with anyone who shares our vision. As our members succeed, NTi succeeds. Likewise, as NTi succeeds, our members, our charities, and our communities succeed. With the right members and with the right meeting leaders, we can and will change the world for the better.

Was Networking Today International the Chicken or the Egg?

In closing, you may be wondering what ever happened to fanplicity... that's another interesting and unexpected positive consequence of my intentionally starting NTi; every single one of fanplicity's products and services now service the needs of NTi – every one of them. fanplicity offers light print work, we need that at NTi. Fanplicity offers web design and development services, we need that at NTi almost daily! NTi constantly needs graphic design work for a variety of web and print demands, and, you guessed it, fanplicity provides those services. NTi needed a robust communication platform that would allow every meeting leader an effective tool for communicating with members and visitors via text and email, and fanplicity's product, FanZooma provides the perfect communication solution! You see, I hope you'll take just a moment to let this sink in: I started NTi to meet the needs of fanplicity, but now fanplicity exists to meet the needs of NTi. Would you call this an unintentional positive consequence of an intentional action? I WOULD!

What do I hope you've gained from my chapter? Did you see how NTi was started intentionally to help fanplicity, but the unintended positive consequence was something more wonderful than I could have ever planned? We must take action to do something, and when we do, good things can and will happen, but I hope you can see that they will not happen by themselves. Realize that things don't always work out the way you plan, and that is okay! Understand you must never give up trying to achieve your dream; that, even though you may not be able to see it, your dream just might be waiting for you right around the next corner! YOU CAN DO IT!

To find an NTi meeting near you or to learn more about starting one, two, or three in your community, find us online at NetworkingTodayIntl.com. By the way, NTi offers revenue sharing compensation for all those that start their own meeting or refers someone to us that successfully launches a meeting. Let's work together to improve our networking, our businesses, our families, and our communities. If nothing else, take this with you: you are just one introduction from changing the course of your own destiny!

ABOUT THE AUTHOR

 Rich DeForest is the creator, founder, and CEO of Networking Today International, Inc., the fastest-growing business networking organization in the world. With decades of experience in sales and marketing, Rich and his team have grown the organization now expanding around the country with more meeting locations being added every week. He also is the President of fanplicity and creator of FanZooma, a communication platform that integrates email and texting as a combined marketing tool. He, his wife and their four children live in Knoxville, Tennessee.

Rich DeForest
CEO Networking Today International
http://NetworkingTodayIntl.com

CHAPTER I

Do Over! How Admitting Defeat Led to Happiness and Success in Our True Calling

By: The Palombi Team, Janet and Dean Palombi

We've all heard the saying, "When life gives you lemons, make lemonade." That's exactly how Janet & Dean, The PALOMBI TEAM, approached life's unexpected twists and turns.

Our thirst for entrepreneurship began on a date night in a coffee shop where we developed our first business venture on a napkin. In 1999, we began our search for a business that would give us more freedom and independence from the cutthroat corporate life that Dean had led and would allow us to spend more time with our kids and each other. We opened a state-of-the-art daycare center, Wee Kids Early Learning Center, in South Jersey. After two years of successfully building our business, we were hit with the impact of the 911 terrorist attacks. Enrollment immediately dropped, and we found ourselves on the brink of bankruptcy.

We had always dreamed of escaping the cold New Jersey winters to live in "sunny, warm Florida," where we had honeymooned and later spent many happy family trips. In pursuit of a fresh start, we sold almost everything we owned - especially our snow shovels! - packed up the car with the kids and the dog and moved south to Florida. We were able to sell the daycare business, but with a huge debt load to pay off, Dean embarked again on a job search in the corporate sales world from which he had earlier fled.

A Fresh Start in Sunny Florida

Once in Florida, we needed a second family car which Dean purchased from a Florida real estate broker who encouraged Dean to consider becoming a realtor and working with his real estate firm. The entrepreneurial spirit ran very strong in our veins. Dean's parents had operated their own hairstyling salon, and Janet's parents, also tired of the corporate world, had owned a Dairy Queen franchise, which they eventually sold when they started a successful business as a husband and wife real estate team in Pennsylvania. Drawing inspiration from both sets of parents, and with time on our hands while Dean searched for a "real job," we decided to follow in Janet's parents' footsteps and obtain our real estate licenses. To our surprise, we found our true calling.

Dean had always thrived in the world of sales, and everyone always thought he was a born salesman who could sell anything and did it quite well. Janet worked in the travel industry and in office management/administration before she became a stay-at-home mom. We had the perfect skill-set combination for starting a real estate business.

We used our marketing skills and Dean began to stand on the corner of a busy Orlando highway at rush hour with a

HUGE sign that simply said, "ASK ME"! People started recognizing him as the "ASK ME" guy and so began our new career. We immediately found moderate success. We moved to a 100% Commission Company in 2002 and soon became the #1 sales and listing team in our office. We maintained top 50 agent status in 2003 with more than $8 million in production, and in 2004 with more than $11 million in production we became the #3 top-selling team company-wide. We focused on southeast Orlando and ranked among the top five agents out of 800 agents for all of 2004 in the 32828 zip code area where we lived, worked, and played. We had no other team members so by keeping focused on one area, we were able to give top-notch service to our customers. About 70% of our business came from referrals and repeat customers.

The secret to our success has been hard work, easy accessibility, and constant interaction with customers many of whom became some of our closest friends. For example, one family came from the United Kingdom and after we sold them their home they became some of our dearest friends.

Orlando's unique position as a top travel destination draws investors from all over the world. Because we were experts in both residential and investment real estate, we put our money where our mouth was. If we invested in a project, our investor buyers would jump in alongside of us. Most of our investors relied upon us to help them resell and quickly turn these properties into a modest gain.

We eventually bought a waterfront townhome in Tampa Bay and sold another in the same community to one of our investor clients. This investment allowed us to grow our business in a new marketplace. We had fallen in love with boating and the Tampa Bay area and this second home investment purchase allowed us to specialize in another area. We now lived, worked, and played in Southeast Orlando and the Tampa Bay marketplace.

The Crash That Led To A Do Over

Poised to take our career to the next level we took a bold leap in 2007 and opened our own Brokerage, Palombi Realty. Our plans came to a screeching halt, however, when the market crashed in 2008. The Florida real estate market took a serious hit and so did we. Our income dropped drastically, and we were at risk of losing our primary home, our second home, an investment property and our business. It was again time for a do over. Our son Kevin, now a senior in high school had visited East Tennessee for a Young Life trip and our daughter Gina, a college student in Florida was considering attending the University of Tennessee. We had friends from our old church in New Jersey who had relocated to Seymour, Tennessee several years prior and they loved living in the Knoxville area. We decided to visit East Tennessee and fell in love with it, too. After eight years of turning lemons into Florida lemonade we decided to make the transition to Tennessee Orange (the color of the much-loved University of Tennessee Volunteers located in Knoxville, in case you're not familiar!).

Dean immediately secured his Tennessee Real Estate Brokers license and Janet soon joined him in obtaining her license. Unfortunately, the downward trend in the Florida market had taken a serious toll on our family finances. Entrepreneurship had hit us hard and we were forced to file bankruptcy. Our son, Kevin, was just starting college and our daughter, Gina, was continuing her college education at the University of Tennessee. Dean had no choice but to re-enter the corporate world and Janet was also faced with the struggle of finding a new career.

Through networking, Janet was presented with several opportunities to work in magazine publication advertising sales which she absolutely hated. She then started her own business in health and fitness, Totally Fit Lifestyle. Janet's passion for health and fitness is what originally launched our day care center. She had a business in New Jersey called Wee Work Out where she provided a fitness and nutrition program to local area day care centers. With Dean, we eventually grew this business into Wee Kids Early Learning Center and Wee Work Out remained a part of our curriculum.

Dean began a career in telecommunications and quickly rose to the top in his field. Unfortunately, his income had capped at 50% of what our income had been in real estate back in Florida. He was presented with the opportunity to change fields and took a job in the heating/air conditioning industry.

A God Thing

We had continued to dabble in real estate the entire time Dean was working in the corporate world, but we eventually put our licenses on voluntary inactive status in order to focus more on our corporate careers. But we could not shake our love and passion for the business. We missed working together, neither of us were loving what we were doing, and the corporate grind was beginning to take a toll on our marriage. In 2016, we decided to seriously work in real estate together again on weekends while Dean continued his corporate job during the week. Janet reactivated our Facebook and LinkedIn business pages, which notified everyone on social media that The Palombi Team was back in action. What we did not realize was that Dean's colleagues in his corporate job were also notified. This created confusion at work and within 24 hours Dean immediately found himself in front of the owner of the company explaining that he was not planning to leave the company, but we had simply reactivated our licenses and social media marketing. The management team asked questions that were right on the money. They said, "We are not sure you can do real estate part time and still do what you do for us. And so, you are going to have to make a choice." That led to some negotiations and it was decided that Dean could stay on there but not be visible as a real estate professional on social media.

In the coming weeks we prayed earnestly about where we were headed and were faced with continuing challenges performing Dean's primary job and selling real estate. The conversation played over and again in Dean's head, "How can you do this job part time? Maybe the boss is right." We lamented and prayed about it. Sure, Dean was making a good income, he loved the people he worked for, and he respected them immensely. So, it was a big mental and emotional battle. Never did he want to bring harm to them or deceive them.

The next week a friend invited Dean to The Hill, a prayer luncheon that he thought was going to be a networking event. To his surprise, it turned out to be an afternoon church service with a great sermon. Dean lingered after the service to talk to his friend and the pastor. While they spoke, most attendees had left the building except for a woman in the back praying aloud over a group of several people. Dean says she reminded him of a character in the "War Room" movie. If you are not familiar with the movie, this fascinating little woman prays in her closet, which she calls "the war room." Dean felt compelled to meet her but was unable to reach her before she disappeared. On his way to his car he was stopped by a woman that held her hand out and asked if she could pray with him. It turned out to be the same woman he had wanted to meet! She prayed, "This man is wrestling with something. He has got to deal with it. I don't know what it is, but I know you have called me to pray with him today and he is going to take action in your name."

Immediately after this powerful and miraculous moment, Dean called Janet and said, "We have to take the leap of faith, go back to real estate full time, and I need to leave my job." Though fearful, Janet agreed, and Dean promptly resigned from his current job.

In hindsight, we realize that the failure of our daycare center ushered in our greatest success. When we moved to Florida we were emotionally and financially bankrupt and we had only two choices: cry over spilled milk or clean up the mess. Our career in Florida allowed us to completely pay off our debt from our first business loss. The misfortune of failure a second time during the 2008 market crash scarred us deeply. But our fierce entrepreneurial spirit and desire for independence from corporate life were the driving factors that originally led us to the world of real estate.

What It Is Like Being In Business With Your Spouse

People ask what it's like working with your spouse. Most of the time it is awesome! Janet's Mom and Dad worked together for many years, so she saw that kind of relationship up close and personal growing up. We do have our moments when we get tired of being together 24/7, but most of the time we love it. Dean says, "When she gets tired of being around me, she sends me out to distribute flyers and knock on doors. I still do this!"

We have our areas of expertise. Dean is great at cold calling and contracts and Janet is great with buyers and social media and the management side of the business. We have learned that if we stick to the areas we are good at and don't tread on each other's toes too much we do pretty well together.

We like the yoke analogy. Two horses can pull harder after being yoked together than any individual horse can pull on their own. That's how we feel about working together. We are stronger together than we could ever be on our own.

Our daughter Gina, son-in-law Brad, son Kevin, and Janet's parents have now all settled in the Knoxville area. The longing to regain our freedom to set our own schedules and enjoy time with family drove us back to our roots. We have chosen to move forward with our business and our lives following these wise words from one of our favorite motivational speakers. "Failing forward is the ability to get back up after you have been knocked down, learn from your mistakes, and move forward in a better direction." – John Maxwell

We have chosen to run our business and live our lives following the words of another favorite motivational speaker, Zig Ziglar who says: "You cannot tailor-make the situations in life, but you can tailor-make the attitudes that fit those situations." And to Zig Ziglar's notion that "Success and happiness are not destinations, they are exciting never-ending journeys," we plan to continue on this journey for a very long time.

ABOUT THE AUTHORS

Janet and Dean Palombi are the dynamic real estate duo of Knoxville known as the PALOMBI TEAM. They are both licensed realtors and have significant experience and success working with both buyers and sellers of residential and investment properties. To date, they have sold almost 500 homes and closed more than $50 million in business throughout their career. They provide an independent and unique style of marketing through their exclusive 6/5/4 program that elevated them to the top 5% in the Florida marketplace. They are a dedicated husband and wife team that provides top-notch service to all their customers through hard work, easy accessibility, and constant interaction. They are excited to work with both buyers and sellers of residential property. Visit their website MakeItaPalombuy.com and Contact them for all of your real estate needs. When You BUY or SELL... Make it a PAL-OM-BUY!

Janet and Dean,
THE PALOMBI TEAM at Realty Executives
865-317-3765
makeitapalombuy@gmail.com
makeitapalombuy.com
facebook.com/MakeitaPalombuy/
linkedin.com/in/janetpalombi

CHAPTER 2

Financial Services and Primerica Removed My Golden Handcuffs

By: Dano Deck

Growing up in the country, I spent my early years working on farms, bailing hay, mowing yards, doing construction, and whatever we had to do to earn spending money. Nothing was ever handed to us kids, so we had to go out and get what we wanted with our own hard work. While in and out of college, I had two to three jobs at a time, like working in clubs and bartending at night, and then construction during the day. I also like horses and wanted to ride, so I worked in the stables and I got to ride for free. It was hard work because I was always busy, but I also earned the money I wanted and found a way to do the things I really wanted to do.

Choosing to Wear the Golden Handcuffs

In 1995, while living in Indiana, I began working in proprietary education for a for-profit college. As a recruiter, it was my job to sit down with students who wanted to go to college, find out what path they wanted to follow for their lives, and go from there with helping them select an area of study at the school. In education they don't call what I was doing "sales," but "recruiting," although the skills and requirements of a sales person and a recruiter are identical.

I eventually spent a total of 16 years in that industry. The great part about working in proprietary education was as I advanced, it became very lucrative, as you might imagine with any sales kind of job. Recruiters can make a lot of money, grow, and advance in their careers, which I was blessed to be able to accomplish.

But it got to the point where like a lot of corporate jobs, the further up the ladder I climbed the more they owned my time. It felt like they created and owned my entire lifestyle. They dictated where I was going to live, how I was going to live, and how much time I spent with my family, which wasn't much time at all. It got to the point where a "light" work week for me was 65 - 75 hours, and the average workweek was around 80 - 90 hours. I lived my life in 12 week-increments at a time, quota to quota, to make sure the numbers were there. It was exhausting and lonely. I missed my wife and our family.

When I moved from Indiana to Tennessee it was to get a break from the grind, except that lasted less than two months because the person I was supposed to replace didn't get the promotion they were promised. And then the person I wanted to work for got fired. So, I went from the frying pan right back into the fire in a leadership position, still doing recruiting. As a director, the recruiting year was my focus. Because the school is open six days a week, and it was my job to make sure it was full every one of those days, I was responsible for new students coming in as well as keeping the students already enrolled. It felt almost like I was on call 24 hours a day, seven days a week and a type of situation where I was always working.

Maybe you've heard of an adage about wearing "golden handcuffs." Golden handcuffs imply you make really, REALLY good money. The more money you make, the more you adjust your lifestyle, which in my case made me justify what I felt like I had to do - work all the time. Those golden handcuffs kept me shackled to doing too much work for a lot of money but at a cost.

I was willing to give up my family and my freedom. From the time I moved to Tennessee in 2005, I didn't go on a spring break or any other kind of family vacation until 2009 when I finally quit working in education. Spring break always happens during my March birthday, but for me, my birthdays were spent alone, by myself, and working while my family was at the beach. I could afford to pay for them to have that lifestyle, but it was always without me there. We had the nice house and the nice cars and the family could have nice vacations (without me of course), but I was working all the time to be able to keep up with that lifestyle.

After years of living - or not living - that lifestyle, I felt burned out. I wondered why I was getting up every day and continually doing work work work work work. Yet, I was almost addicted to the stress and those golden handcuffs again... the more money I made the more things I wanted to buy. I had to get the bigger house, the better cars, and on and on. Eventually I realized none of it satisfies.

Although I was working to acquire more things, I didn't have the time to fully enjoy the things. I got to enjoy my car while I commuted back and forth to the job which had already worn me out. I got to go home and sleep in the house that I go to work to pay for, so I can enjoy it, but I didn't get to enjoy it because I was not there most of the time. It was that kind of mundane existence and a lifestyle a lot of people making a "good living" fall victim to. I knew there had to be a better way. Something else. But I didn't know how to go from what I was doing, and what I perceived was a great lifestyle to start, in essence, a whole new lifestyle a whole new career.

"I Want Your Job!"

During a rare moment of personal time away from my job, I was working with a couple of pastors of a small church plant who hosted a men's Bible study. I met this gentleman who was living a lifestyle I couldn't even believe was possible. He did something with finance, but I wasn't sure exactly what, so I asked him about it. I said, "Hey I've got some investments I need to do something with and I'd like to bounce some ideas off you."

He came over to the house and I showed him what I wanted to do financially, and we were on the same page. It was pretty simple. I had to take money that was only growing a little bit and turn it into a supplement of the cash flow which came from the adjustment in the positions I experienced when I moved to Tennessee in those first couple of months. As it was, I had the wrong kind of insurance plans, and debt from mortgages. He showed me how much faster I could pay off those bills, fully fund college for my kids, and realign my cash flow and assets into the things that work for me. I discovered for the first time exactly how money worked. I now had a plan with an end goal. That's how I first experienced Primerica.

When everything was said and done, I asked him what I had to do to have his job. I remember him saying, "Why would you want my job? You wouldn't want my job. You've got a great career with 13 years in the company and one of the highest paid at your level." But he had that lifestyle - I'm telling you the man golfed all the time. Now, I'd never swung a club, but I know playing golf means a lot of time doing what you want. To me it would mean time on the lake outside with my family and doing things I could barely even enjoy on a weekend (remember I worked Monday - Friday and on Saturdays, too), let alone whenever I wanted.

For me it was easy: I wanted more money and I wanted more time. The problem is, usually people can get one of those, but they've got to give up the other. Call me greedy, but I wanted both money and time. When I saw Primerica would allow me to achieve exactly what I wanted, I was in.

Because the guy who mentored me was doing well where he was, he set some high goals and challenged me. He told me, "You've got to get trained and go get your licenses and some field training all in the next two weeks or I'm not going to waste my time with you." My first week in the industry, I went to licensing class, and within two weeks I had my first license. Then I went out in the field meeting with some neighbors who were strangers and learned how to do some presentations.

As I learned the business of financial services, I started in my very spare time, which was about three hours a week on Saturday afternoons from about 3:00 to 6:00 PM. I jumped into it, got my licenses, and learned how to build a business. As I understood more what I needed to do to become successful, I wondered how I could put more time and effort into growing my business. Meanwhile, the pressures at my job grew and the stress levels grew, too. As I came to see how I could become very successful with Primerica, for a while I burned the candle at both ends and ultimately figured out an exit strategy.

It's Time to Get Married

In 2007 I went to the Primerica International Convention in the Georgia Dome in Atlanta. I met a number of different people from the business and saw the bigger picture of what the company was all about, what you could do, where you could go, and I realized it was unlimited opportunity. What I always wanted: THIS was it. They showed me the proverbial carrot. And if I did what I needed to do I could go as far as I wanted to go. So right then and there I decided, I'm all in. I told my wife, "We can't date this thing anymore. It's time to get married to it!" So, we jumped in and got after it.

I made a goal and gave myself two years from then, which would have been the summer of 2009, to replace my income and quit my job. On April 1st of 2009 I fired my boss and walked away from it all a few months ahead of schedule. I love every minute of my work with Primerica today. It's allowed me to have the freedom I want with my family. And as a result, I go after whatever goals and dreams I want to reach and today I get to play hard.

Speaking of Being Married... Shared Goals Make You Unstoppable

My wife, Heather, came into the business to support me back in 2007 just before attending our first convention together. She's been an amazing partner, whether it's keeping things going on the home front or whatever needs to be done managing the office, planning for meetings and trainings and other important tasks that must be done. With Heather handling the office tasks, I can stay focused out in the field working with clients, or recruiting and training, and developing our people in the field.

Some people assume it's challenging to work with family. But I ask them, "When's the last time you tried it?" I think if you've got two people, whether they're married or they're family or however related, if you've got common goals and you're working towards the same thing, you as a team can become unstoppable. When you both know where you want to go and what you want to do, then why not be supportive to get those things and make it come into fruition.

We Never Chase the Accolades, But...

After going full time with the business in 2009, Heather and I became regional vice presidents back in 2011. In 2015, we won a Power Builder Award and were given a watch. In 2017, we became members of the Financial Independence Council and were awarded six-figure rings. We've been top recruiters, top producers, and did well in all areas of the business at different times. But we never chase the accolades as much as we want to have the freedom to have fun with the family and do the things that corporate America never allowed me to do. While reaching for our personal goals of being together and providing for our family, the awards and things naturally followed.

Smashing the No

You can chase income and be miserable. The biggest thing is if I'd known how much fun life can be with the trips and the experiences which are out there waiting, maybe I would have gone after it quicker to be able to experience more of all the good experiences in life sooner.

If you realize the "no" from potential clients isn't so painful, you'd just go ahead and get them all out of the way fast as you could. But those "no's" are never permanent. It's really more like "next opportunity." I've been in the business 16 plus years now. I've got people who were the most adamant "no's" in the world who are now the best clients I've ever had. It's because life changes and situations change. In the early stages some people are just trying to see what you're made of. I knew if I stuck it out long enough, they would know they can count on me for what I was saying I could do.

What it boils down to for me is I'm too bull-headed to quit. Once I put my mind to it, I stick with it, don't get discouraged, and have thick skin. Buddies of mine always say, "Man you've got that strong work ethic," but I think, "Compared to what?" Growing up shoveling literal crap and bailing hay, doing construction, now that's hard work. Today I don't even work up a sweat! It's about being consistent, knowing the goal, and working the plan to get it done. Does a "no" hurt your back so you can't work in the morning? Did you smash your "no" so you can't walk? Find your resilience and go after what you want.

ABOUT THE AUTHOR

 A nine-time college dropout, Dano Deck finally earned multiple degrees in both business and in Biblical studies. He is an ordained minister and has volunteered with various church plants, revamps, and has led small groups, performed weddings, and mentored others. Starting his career in financial services for Primerica in 2006, Dano Deck has earned numerous awards, becoming regional vice president and a member of the Financial Independence Council. Married to Heather since 1995, he is the father of two young men and one daughter and they make their home in Knoxville, Tennessee. You can reach Dano at: 865-771-1226 to learn more about Primerica.

CHAPTER 3

Remodeling Life for Success

By: Vince Thompson

I was introduced to the building trades when I was about 10 years old. My dad purchased 12 acres in the country in central Ohio and along with my great uncle who is a master carpenter, designed and built an earth-sheltered home. If you're not familiar with an earth-sheltered home, it's a unique structure that is built into the land either completely submerged underground, partially underground, or "bermed" with earth covering one or more walls. It was such a great place to grow up as a young boy with 12 acres of woods, fields, and a creek. I can remember "helping" out by climbing around the building site, playing in the creek, and on occasion, carrying a few two by fours.

Fast forward to the summer of my 10th grade in high school, where I was lucky enough to grab a job at the local seed farm and helped out by working in the fields and learning how to make handyman repairs around the farm. The farm owner was kind enough to keep me on each summer for the next several years.

I took a year off between high school and college when I landed a job with a local log home builder. I worked that year and every break during the first two years of college, until I decided to drop out of college because my father passed away. After the death of my father I continued with the same log home builder for another year until I got married.

My dad wore more hats than just those of a husband and father to four kids. In 1970, he started an automotive repair business that is still thriving to this day. As if that weren't enough, he planted a church (in the garage of the home he built) when I was in the sixth grade. After my dad passed away, our church joined with another local church, which provided us with a pastor.

I quickly got to know the new pastor, Jay, and he soon offered me a job working for his family hot tub service business. After working for Jay for a year or so he approached me with an offer to sell me his business. It took some financial wrangling and a lot of prayers, but my new wife and I managed to get approved for a loan to buy what would be the first of many businesses! I was only 23 years old, newly married, and now I was self-employed as well. After the ups and downs that come with a couple of years of self-employment and throwing a newborn son into the mix, I decided to explore the options of selling the business and taking a job with a different spa and hot tub company.

"You don't learn by following the rules. You learn by doing and by falling over.

Do not be embarrassed by your failures, learn from them and start again."
- Richard Branson

Hiring a professional to help with polishing my resume, I started my search and was quickly invited to East Tennessee to interview with a spa manufacturer that was expanding into Knoxville. Shortly after the interview I was offered a job as the service manager and it was going to be time to move my wife and infant son to a state where we didn't know a single soul.

During the job search I had been putting the word out about wanting to sell our business and was approached by a family member who expressed an interest in buying it. When it became clear that my wife, son, and I would be moving from our home in Ohio to Tennessee, the family member and I reached a handshake agreement and the sale was set to take place shortly after our move. Now, being young, dumb, and inexperienced, I forwent a written contract for the sale of the business or even a letter of intent, which proved to be a mistake. Several weeks after moving to Knoxville the family member changed their mind about buying the business. Of course, I was counting on the money from the sale of the business to pay off the remainder of the business loan and have a little left over to help get established in a new city! Suddenly I had none of the money, all of the debt, and no way to pay the business bills. Looking back with 20/20 hindsight and a couple of decades of business experience, I would have done things much differently.

Unfortunately, the broken deal launched my wife and I into what we often refer to as "our season of hell." My new job did not provide enough income to cover both our living expenses and the expenses from the spa business, still mine back in Ohio. As you can imagine it wasn't long before the collection calls started coming in for the business debt. We held on for several months before we had no choice but to file bankruptcy. In fact, by that time we were so broke we had to borrow money to even pay our bankruptcy attorney!

As if bankruptcy wasn't stressful enough there was trouble with the new job. The planned expansion into Knoxville hit some snags and I was moved from service manager to service tech. Shortly after that demotion I left that company.

Some time passed, another job came and went, and then in 2007, I found employment with a company that was on the leading edge of much of the revitalization happening in downtown Knoxville. To say I learned a lot at that company would be a huge understatement. As everyone knows the years 2007 to 2009 were difficult for anyone in the building trades and our company was no exception. Several things conspired together and in October of 2008 I was invited to no longer be associated with that company. Two months before Christmas at the start of a recession was not a great time to become unemployed. To add to the "excitement," by this time my wife and I had purchased our first home two weeks before the birth of our second son, who was at that point four years old.

A few days into my unemployment I had a moment of epiphany and thought, "I can do this myself!" So, I launched back into the adventure of self-employment. The first job on my own was a buildout for an architect in downtown Knoxville. He had purchased a studio apartment and had a highly custom design in mind. I ended up working on his project for nearly a year as he had hidden trap doors, full extension drawers built into steps, moveable walls, and reclaimed brick pillars along with many other unique and custom ideas I made into reality.

For several years after that (remember, this was during 2008-2009 in a terrible economy, especially for builders) my business struggled to gain any traction. If it weren't for both my mother and mother-in-law living with us at that time, I'm not sure we would have made it financially.

Networking and Connections Made the Difference

As I struggled to keep my new business going, I remembered my dad had attended a few Christian Business Men's International meetings for both his business and our church. There isn't a CBMI chapter in Knoxville, but I found a local Christian business networking group and joined up. Not much came of that group but it piqued my interest in business networking. Shortly after the Christian business group dissolved, I discovered and joined another local networking group called REO. It was a stretch for me to pay the membership and monthly fees, but I knew it was a necessary growth step for me and my business. Being involved in that organization taught me a lot and I'm still friends with the leader and several members to this day. After a year or so of attending the REO networking meetings I could tell it was time to move on and I joined a local BNI chapter. It wasn't long until I connected with a realtor who kept me busy with everything from handyman jobs to full blown remodels. The work was great, but I just never reached the level I needed to really "make it". It was in that BNI chapter that I made one of two connections that eventually put me into the business I have today.

The first connection was more of an introduction to another style of networking group or a mastermind / think tank group for business owners. You know the formula: gather 10-12 business owners in a room with a wise and experienced leader and you share your struggles, victories and defeats while learning from each other. The second connection was with a new networking group called Networking Today. Around that same time, I developed an interest in insurance-based work from water damage and started looking into what it would take to make that a part of my business.

While attending a Networking Today meeting I started talking to a HVAC contractor who had a client that needed a few small things done and was thinking about converting a deck into a sunroom. I visited with this client (Rick) and won the job. As I was working on the job and talking to Rick I shared that I was looking into insurance restoration as a way of expanding my business. Little did I know at that time Rick had invested in other small businesses and was wanting to do so again. He was in the process of selling a sporting goods business that he had started in New York and let me know that as soon as that sale was complete, he wanted to review my business plan and would consider investing in my business. I worked and polished my business plan until I felt it was perfect. Several months later Rick and

I met, and he gave me a check to fund the expansion of my business!

Although I considered a franchise model, and even traveled to Los Angeles to check it out, ultimately, I decided against become a franchise owner due to the large financial burden and struck out on my own. I spent a week in Atlanta getting licensed and certified and then on Valentine's Day my wife and I drove to Nashville to pick up our new business trailer and new equipment. How romantic!

The marketing was in place, the networking was in place, and it didn't take long for the phone to ring. My first restoration job was for a church whose choir room flooded from a malfunction in the HVAC unit on the roof. I continued working restoration jobs as they came in as well as remodel and repair jobs but still wasn't quite making it.

Through my networking activities, I was introduced to another business owner who'd been a general contractor for 17 years. Dawn and I talked on the phone and met at a Starbucks (where else do business owners meet?). I remember feeling very excited to meet her because she's something of a minor local celebrity. I had seen her company trucks around town and listened to her host a home improvement themed show called "Around the House" on the local talk radio station for several years.

> *"The difference between successful people &*
> *very successful people is that very successful*
> *people say 'no' to almost everything."*
> - **Warren Buffet**

Dawn and I shared with each other what we were each looking for related to our individual businesses and decided that the timing wasn't right to do anything together. I left the meeting feeling disappointed and wasn't sure where to go from there.

But, about a month later the same networking colleague who introduced me to Dawn, called me and said that he had another "team up" idea. This time it involved two other business owners and the merging of our businesses. Dawn happened to be one of the other two business owners. After several meetings, we decided to merge our companies and form a new business. Between the three of us we would be able to offer remodeling, new home construction, roofing and insurance restoration.

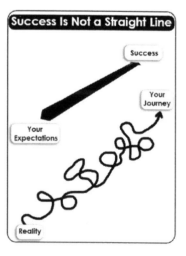

We moved into a joint office and started on our new venture. But something didn't seem right. It took a while, but in my role as the general manager, I was able to start tracking down some of our issues. It became apparent that what the three of us offered as home builders and home remodelers was not compatible for us in our situation, so Dawn and I left that joint venture and started our own company in January of 2017.

Our company, Master Remodelers, now focuses on remodeling kitchens and bathrooms and providing what we call a "Masterpiece Level Experience." We do things like take our clients shopping with a designer and teach free seminars on remodeling and design trends. Together Dawn and I have just shy of forty years' experience in the building trades. We're always learning and are seeking ways to improve.

My business worldview has been rocked over the last three years. I've been fortunate to learn on the job two of the most crucial aspects of running a successful business: (1) the importance business systems and (2) pricing to make a profit. When you implement the right systems and understand all the details that need to go into how you price a job, success will follow.

Since I was 23 years old I've started several businesses, lost one, declared bankruptcy, closed two, merged another and started my current LLC / Partnership.

I have a picture taped to my desk that looks something like this image.

I've discovered that "success" or "making it" is something that truly doesn't exist or if it does, it looks much different than most people believe. I'm trying to learn to enjoy the journey.

"Your word is a lamp unto my feet, and a light to my path." - Psalm 119:105

In looking at one of my favorite Bible verses, it's important to realize that a lamp isn't very useful in the light. A lamp is most useful when the light is low, and times are dark. The Bible never promises us a smooth and easy path, it just promises us that Jesus will be with us.

Through all the ups and downs, the hopes and dreams, the victories and the defeats there have been a few constants:

1. The church may have failed me, but Jesus never has.
2. My wife and children have always supported me.
3. I've never stayed "given up."

Today I have a great business partner from whom I'm always learning, and I can see many opportunities ahead for the business, myself, and my family.

ABOUT THE AUTHOR

 Vince is a third-generation entrepreneur who works with homeowners to craft a Masterpiece remodel. Having been self-employed the majority of his career, Vince has grown to believe that working for yourself is one of the best, hardest, and most rewarding things that someone could do. Over the course of his life Vince has owned and/or started several businesses with the majority being in a remodeling related field. Vince has held certifications in hoarding clean-up, water, fire and mold remediation. He is also a licensed contractor and an Age Safe America Senior Home Safety Specialist. He has been a guest on two local radio shows and a local podcast talking about remodeling and business. However, the most important things in his life are his faith in Christ, his wife of twenty-four years, and his two sons. He lives in the country in East Tennessee where he enjoys walks with his wife, nerdy activity with his oldest son, and hunting with his youngest son. In his spare time, he can often be found on his back deck or front porch.

Vince Thompson
Owner / Partner Master Remodelers
RemodelingKnoxville.com
Vince@RemodelingKnoxville.com
(office) 865-458-0416
(cell) 865-805-9714

CHAPTER 4

From Shy Wallflower to Master Connector

By: Sharon Cawood

People who know me today have a difficult time believing I was a very shy person growing up and as a young adult, but it's true. My first college degree was in accounting and then later in life I earned a bachelor's degree in Organizational Management and a master's degree in Corporate Adult Education (HRD). Most of my early career was spent in the accounting field, in an office environment. I was not expected to network outside the company - networking wasn't even a term I was familiar with.

While working on my bachelor and master's degrees, I also worked for a human resource organization that specialized in helping companies manage workforce downsizing. I began working for this company as an office manager/accountant and transitioned into a sales position while working on my degrees.

In the new sales position, I was the first person a client's employee would meet with just after being terminated from their job. So, I felt like the "angel of death" when somebody was laid off. After they were given the bad news, I was the next person they saw, and it was my job to connect them with the consultant who would work with them through finding a new position.

Formal business networking was not really a "thing" that sales people did in East Tennessee - I don't remember any business networking groups around back then. At that point, part of my job was to know all the human resources people in East Tennessee. These were the folks making decisions about company downsizings. And that's how I got into networking. I had transitioned from an accounting position into a sales position. My endeavor was to get to know all the human resource people in East Tennessee because that was the territory my company wanted me to cover. But back then, I was so shy, I had a hard time talking with anyone I didn't know. Just walking up and starting a conversation with folks who were strangers was very difficult for me, but I knew that was something about myself I needed to change. I remember one morning as I was walking from the parking lot into my office I thought, "OK... I've got to start working on this."

Shy Wallflower No More

From then on, each morning during my walk into the office and each afternoon on my way out of the office I decided to speak to at least one person; one in the morning and one in the afternoon. As I started doing that, it became a habit of talking to somebody whenever I was coming and going. It began easily enough. I'd practice starting little conversations. For example, as I was going on the elevator, or walking down the hall, or headed to the break room, I'd simply say,

"Good morning! How are you?" or "How was your day? My office is in the south tower, where's yours?" That's what got me away from being an extremely shy wallflower.

Outside of the office, I still had to meet those human resources people. I'd joke with friends that I had three lunches a day to get a chance to sit down with enough human resources professionals so I could get to know them and have them get to know me. Most days, I'd have three back-to-back lunch meetings set up: one at 11 AM, one at Noon, and one at 1:00 PM. All those lunches allowed me to get out there meeting people as a business professional for the first time in my life. That's how I learned about the power of connecting with people and networking plus how to eat three lunches a day and not gain weight! Over the years I started building my personal database of connections, which I still use today.

Business networking was beginning to bud in East Tennessee and my company developed a way to gather the folks we needed to consistently be in front of and cultivate relationships with by hosting breakfast and lunch group meetings. We offered interesting topics, excellent speakers, and the opportunity for them to get to know each other too. It was a win-win for everyone - thus began our networking group.

Over the years, I worked with several startup companies writing business plans, teaching career skills, and migrating through the dot com years where most of the positions I held included the need for some sort of networking to be successful.

Around 2007, I had the honor of serving the sixth district of Knox County as their County Commissioner for about year. My job was to connect with my constituents and represent their interests to the government and focus on making decisions based on what was right for the community. Whenever an issue would come up, my main concern, and what determined my votes every time was what I thought was right for the people in my district and Knox County as a whole.

During my time on County Commission my database of contacts grew exponentially. Constituents would call me, and I would work with them to help them get their issues resolved with the government. I added all of those folks to my database of people and kept notes so I could refer and help them later, if needed. I was building relationships and networking to serve the community.

After my time as a Commissioner, I went on to work with Welcome Wagon®. In case you're not familiar with the company, Welcome Wagon®, a subsidiary of Move.com was founded to connect new homeowners with businesses in their community that could provide them services that someone moving into a community may need. My Welcome Wagon® territory included 14 areas in East Tennessee including all the contiguous counties around Knox County. My job was to find the best businesses to recommend to the new families moving into the communities. I spent my days meeting with business owners, getting to know them and working with them to make their marketing program with Welcome Wagon® successful. I used business networking and relationship building to give and receive leads and referrals to the best companies.

The Imploding Database of Connections

As much as anything else, I've really become more of a master connector. The reason is because I genuinely care about people. Over the years, as I have built my large database of people I've met at one time or another, I may not necessarily remember every detail about every person, but I keep notes on the important information about them and then I can introduce folks to the right people when the time comes.

When you are building your list of connections, it is important to be consistent with the way you populate your database. Use both first and last name. I have several people with the same name now and need to designate them by job title! Insert company names, cell phone number, office email addresses, and of course mailing addresses. Keep notes in your database. Those are often helpful if you need to search to find someone but cannot remember their name.

At this point, I have a contact list of somewhere between 3000 - 4000 people that I've personally met over the course of time. Because I've kept meticulous data and notes, when someone needs a referral to a certain company, for example, all I have to do is pull up my database to make the introduction. Of course, your data will only be as good as you are about updating the information. People change jobs, move, retire and even die. Keep your database up to date as their names, phone numbers and other information often change. Using a business card scanning software is a helpful way to quickly get new contacts into your database.

I'm involved with several networking groups and sometimes a person may say, "I need to get into Pilot. Who do you know at Pilot?" Because I have a good database of my connections, I can pull up Pilot to see who I know there, and I'll get a list of everyone I know at Pilot. At large organizations I try to also keep information about which department each person works in. That's even more helpful when you can refer someone directly into the department they need to reach.

How did this massive database get started? It all started with a simple Excel spreadsheet to keep track of the details. Over time it has grown significantly, and at some point, that Excel file almost imploded. My Excel file of contacts was eventually converted to Outlook and then when I outgrew Outlook I converted everything to the Mac email client.

Once smart phones were introduced along with the ability to store all this data on the cloud life got easier with managing this big database. Then I discovered how easy it is to coordinate my database with my Gmail calendar and Gmail, so today that's how it's all connected, and I can simply use my phone and my laptop - both sync with each other so the data is always at hand. I don't have to worry about my computer or phone crashing or corrupting the data because the details are all in the cloud where I can easily access it from anywhere at a moment's notice and to make those strategic connections and introductions right on the spot.

Moving to N2 Publishing and Meeting MORE Local Business Owners

After several years at Welcome Wagon®, my director there discovered N2 Publishing and called to tell me about the company. She was so excited about it, she connected me with Earl Seals, who is the president of N2 Publishing. Earl happens to be from Morristown, Tennessee, just outside of Knoxville, so he knows the Knoxville community and when we met he was eager to launch the Knoxville market.

As soon as I read the business plan for N2 Publishing, and when I saw the social event aspect of what N2 does I remember thinking, "This is a no brainer!" Every business owner I meet with every day wants to get in front of the people they would like to have as clients, have dinner with them, and get to know them to build relationships, which allows them to grow their businesses. People do business with the folks they know, like and trust.

The way N2 works is we publish private monthly newsletters that contain stories about the residents in the affluent neighborhoods we serve along with other related neighborhood news. In addition to the printed newsletters, we also host social events for the neighborhood and our newsletter sponsors (advertisers) are invited to attend. The

N2 marketing program offers a way for the sponsors to build their word-of-mouth referrals in the neighborhoods.

Across the country, N2 publishes about 1,000 newsletters each month; I own the franchise for Knoxville, Tennessee. The newsletters are well-read because the neighbors themselves write the stories! Our social events are well-attended – we keep an RSVP list and have a waiting list once the seating is full. My sponsors love the opportunity to connect with the residents in the neighborhoods, build relationships and know that when these families need their services they will get a call.

Over the years, publishing the newsletters every month and getting to know the folks who live in my neighborhoods has afforded me the opportunity to become the "go-to person" when a family needs a recommendation of who to call. It is not uncommon for me to get a phone call, text or email asking who I would recommend for them to call. One of the things I try to do with the business owners I'm recommending is give them information about who may be calling them, and I include any information I have about what exactly is needed. My clients know to respond in a timely manner and make sure these folks are given first-class treatment. Happy neighbors are happy customers and happy word-of-mouth referrals for my clients' future customers.

It is important for me to constantly uncover the good businesses in the area and get to know them. I use Networking Today International (NTi) to cultivate these opportunities. Networking doesn't happen at the meetings, it happens after the meetings when we meet and get to know more about each other's business. The better we know each other and our capabilities the better we can focus our referrals. Don't underestimate the power of having coffee with someone to simply learn more about them and their business. You also never know who knows whom – they could be the daughter of the business owner you have been trying to get in front of for months. I learned a long time ago not to pre-judge the folks I have the opportunity to meet every day.

Over the years, I have put together my Power Team – these are the people I most frequently refer folks to. I try to gather my Power Team for lunch several times a year, so they can get to know each other. I feel like if we all know each other we will feed each other. Everyone wants word-of-mouth referrals, and everyone should want to give word-of-mouth referrals.

Connecting Families and Business Owners for a Living

My favorite part of what I get to do is help the business owners I meet to connect with the families in the communities I serve. As I get to meet people around town and folks know I have many connections I am often asked for referrals, which I love to provide. Families in the neighborhoods, friends, my family and even other business owners call me and ask for a recommendation for a good plumber or handyman or contractor. The neighborhoods I serve also have Facebook pages where people ask for recommendations for various projects and so forth and I'm active in those online groups as well. I always give the company name, the owners name and also a phone number. I try to make it as easy as possible for the person to pick up the phone and call the person I'm recommending.

Facilitating those relationships and referrals is such a powerful way to do business for the customer and for the business owner because the customer knows the person I refer is somebody that I personally know and have vetted. And on the other side, the business owner knows this person called me for a referral, so it's somebody who's not messing around – they are a real buyer with a real challenge they need help with. They know the customer needs this and they know I gave the customer the business owner's name and number.

In some cases, I refer those business owners I have used myself in my own home and for my needs. I always tell people if I have worked with someone and what that business did for me. There is one home repair guy who is a fully licensed contractor whom I've used numerous times. He could build an entire home, put on a room addition, handle minor plumbing issues, or fix the roof. Because he can do many different things, I personally hire him often. So, when something comes up I'm happy to refer him. It's very rewarding to be able to call my own personal contractor and say, "Hey I just gave your name to Nancy over in Gettysvue and she should be calling you this afternoon."

ABOUT THE AUTHOR

Sharon Cawood is a franchise owner and the Area Director for N2 Publishing Knoxville, Tennessee. She is a graduate of South College with an ABS degree in accounting. From Tusculum University, Sharon holds a bachelor's degree in organizational management and a Master of Arts in corporate adult education. Sharon has won every golf tournament she's played in because she says she knows how to put a team together (and she's only played in one tournament)! She's a G-mama to seven grand-babies and two grand dogs and makes the best chicken & dumplings EVER. Her hobbies include travel, recipe hunting, golf, classical piano and singing gospel music. You can contact Sharon at Sharon@SharonCawood.com.

CHAPTER 5

Fostering Hope for Foster Kids in Tennessee

By: Allen McMichael

*"For I know the plans I have for you,"
declares the Lord, "plans to prosper you and
not to harm you, plans to give you hope
and a future." Jeremiah 29:11*

In 2013, while on a family vacation with my wife and I, our three adult children, and 12 grandchildren, the idea for Fostering Hope Tennessee was born. It was a rainy day at the lake house and everyone was sitting around the living room just hanging out. As a family, we began discussing what kind of charitable work we could do together. With the size of our family I felt we really could do something special. Our oldest granddaughter, Elizabeth Chanté, was in her mid-20s and the youngest was almost a teenager, so it was the perfect age for them to be involved in giving back and serving the community.

My granddaughter, Elizabeth Chanté Hensley, got the ball rolling. She is a social worker with a master's degree from Boston University and she suggested we do something to reach out to foster kids. I never knew much about how the foster care system worked or anything about the needs of the kids who are in the foster care system. But after graduating from college, my granddaughter worked as a social worker in Boston for a while, and then came back to Knoxville and began working for another social agency called Camelot.

As Chanté told us more about what little the kids in the foster system are able to bring with them when they are placed in foster homes, we knew what we wanted to do. On our brochures there is a photograph of a little girl, carrying a trash bag. That photo wasn't staged. It's a true picture of how that little girl was picked up and taken to another home – with the few belongings and clothing she had stuffed into a plain, black trash bag. The sad reality is a trash bag is all most if not all foster kids have with them at one of the most confusing, scary, and difficult times of their young lives. It's dehumanizing and degrading – and what's worse, kids can feel like they are the ones who did something wrong and that is why they are being removed from their homes so unceremoniously by having whatever toys, books, and clothing the case worker can find stuffed into a trash bag. Imagine feeling like your life's most important possessions are worth nothing more than trash, and you have a sense of how many of these children can feel in that moment.

Our First Project – A $12,000 Request

We knew we could do better. We decided on our focus: Furnishing children in the foster care system with suitcases, backpacks, school supplies, and personal items for their travels between homes.

Right off the bat we knew what we needed to do, and we knew who we needed to do it for because with Chanté's direct experience working with the office of the Department of Child Services (DCS) already, getting started for us was very fast. Our first big project came almost immediately. The DCS folks wanted to know if we could furnish backpacks for an event they hosted with social service agencies from seven counties in East Tennessee. They wanted to supply the children associated with these agencies with backpacks filled with school supplies. They needed about 400 backpacks! What a way to get started with our first fundraising drive!

The children in the foster care system range from newborn to 18 years old and we decided we would put from $25 to $30 worth of school supplies, personal items, teddy bears, or other small toys in the backpack based on various ages. To do that, we needed about $12,000 to make that happen for the first 400 requested, but we had no money coming in. Our foundation runs on a shoestring budget; dollars in equals dollars out. We receive the request, determine what funds and supplies we need, do fundraising to make it happen, use the money for that particular project, and then do it all again.

Soon after we started Fostering Hope and received that request for the 400 backpacks, I joined Networking Today International. Rich, the founder of Networking Today fell in love with our project and felt the need, like we did, to do something to help take care of the foster children we wanted to serve. I told him, "We've got to raise $12,000 to be able to do 400 backpacks." The people in Networking Today opened their hearts and their wallets and jumped right in to help us with that first project and they have been our biggest fundraising supporter ever since.

Back then, though, I wasn't too smart. After we raised the funds, we ordered all 400 backpacks plus all the supplies to fill them from a big box store's online website. We had UPS coming to my house about every day with boxes and boxes of stuff. There was so much! Then, we took it all to our church and we had volunteers pack the backpacks with the supplies. After they were packed, we loaded them into a large portable moving pod storage box (the kind they put on the driveway for people who are moving from house to house), and they stored it until it was time to take the filled backpacks to the event on a specific Saturday. When the pod was delivered, I unloaded the backpacks all myself and sorted them by ages.

After I unloaded the backpacks and organized them, I sat back and watched the kids getting one. They unzipped the bags right then and there and had the biggest smiles on their faces. For some of them, the new backpack was the only thing they own in their life. Foster kids get moved around from seven to ten times in their lifetime. And that day, we gave those kids something they can carry with them wherever they go, from home to home, and beyond.

Doing Things a Better Way

Now we do things differently. When individual people ask to help, I supply the backpack, or they can pick up a backpack at any big box store, we tell them the age of a child, and then say, "Now go fill it up." That makes it better for everybody, including me! We tell people to select school supplies every kid needs like crayons, markers, pencils, pens, notebooks, folders, glue, and so on; personal items based on a child's age such as toothbrush and toothpaste, hair brush and comb, and other small items; and maybe a little something extra - sort of like a Christmas stocking. Some children would like to get a small blanket, for example. If the child is very young, diapers can go into their backpack. People who want to help can involve their children, families, or even Boy Scouts or Girl Scout troops of any ages.

As we really got going, we formed a board of directors, yet still, Fostering Hope Tennessee remains very much a family activity. Both my sons sit on the board, Dr. Jeff McMichael, and Greg McMichael, who played baseball for the Atlanta Braves during the 1990s; also on the board is my sister, Becky Taylor, and my niece, Kristy Bruce. And of course, Elizabeth Hensley, that's my Chanté, sits on the board and is my right-hand partner in the day-to-day operations.

Fundraising with Celebrities and Regular Folks

Each year since 2014 we hold a celebrity golf tournament with the help of my son, Greg, who still works for the Atlanta Braves as a representative for the past players association for the Braves. When sponsors sign up to play in the tournament at the highest level, your team gets assigned a former Braves player to join in their foursome, and then Greg takes the foursome back to Atlanta, gives them a tour of the stadium, and they get tickets to a ball game. And here again, Networking Today members often pay to sponsor a hole, buy banners, and so forth. They are still our biggest supporters.

In November 2017, I felt like God put it on my heart to invite famous Gospel singer, Guy Penrod to town for a concert. He used to be the lead singer for the Gaither Trio, and some years ago stepped out on his own in faith as a solo act, and now he's one of the top tours in that industry. My wife, Sylvia and I heard him sing at Dollywood in the past, love his music, and thought it'd be great to bring him in and invite the foster kids and their families to hear his songs and his message of faith and hope. People thought I was crazy trying to bring in this big celebrity, but I was willing to step out in faith myself and try to make it work. And the more we got to think about it, the more we realized the concert could be a great fundraiser for us.

We decided to hold the event in May 2018 because May is foster care month, so it'd be a perfect fit. Through Networking Today, one of the members offered $1000 match if the organization would be able to raise another $1000 first - and that's just what they did. Hundreds of people came to the concert, and of the hundreds more who wanted to attend but had other commitments on that same night, many simply bought and donated tickets so others could go. It was an amazing night.

A Lifetime of Preparation for Fostering Hope

My professional career started in a Westinghouse warehouse and a little while later, I began selling insurance on the side.

In 1961, I became a full time representative for Metropolitan Life and eventually was promoted to management for 13 years. In 1981 I went into business for myself as an insurance broker; so, I've been selling insurance all my life, and still do to this day. I feel like that experience prepared me for asking people to participate in fundraisers and to volunteer to help us out with Fostering Hope.

When the Affordable Care Act became law, of course the insurance industry changed dramatically, and I lost a good deal of business in all the shifting and changes that occurred, including one company that sold to a larger corporation and lost me $30,000. That's not something selling insurance I could make back overnight. In looking for avenues to pick up the slack, I discovered Legal Shield, which worked well for me as a gap-filler because I could add it as an employer benefit. I also sell ACN cellular phone services. I've been blessed over my career and now running Fostering Hope lets me give back.

Trouble and Trash Bags No More

Our foundation is very much on standby for various agencies who know about us now. For example, recently we did 50 backpacks full of school supplies for a farm in Oak Ridge. Then last week DCS called us because they wanted 25 backpacks. They need something, and we go do it.

Each year we have a Christmas party and then a summer get together for the children in the area. There are about 900 children in foster care in Knoxville and the surrounding areas, so each time these events are a major undertaking, but we love it and so do the kids, who look forward to these special events just for them.

One time we hosted 120 foster kids for a day at the Knoxville Zoo. The zoo gave us a discount, so we could provide free tickets for all the children and their families, which included the zoo admission and a meal for everyone. That turned out to be a $7,000 project. We did some fundraising to be able to provide for that event and again, the people in Networking Today jumped in and were the biggest supporters over the course of a 4-week project to raise what we needed to show the children and the families a nice day at the zoo.

But the biggest impacts don't come from the big events. They come from knowing we helped one child who needed it at a time in their lives when they didn't think they had anything.

One day, at Camelot in Oak Ridge, they had a young woman come in who was on her way to begin her college career. As a foster child, she was able to attend college because the state of Tennessee provides for tuition and a guaranteed education. This young woman came in carrying three trash bags of her only belongings in the world, headed off to college like that. Now, I want you to put your feet in that girl's shoes and you're getting ready to walk into your dormitory at college for the first time with three trash bags with your supplies. How does that feel? We were able to give her nice suitcases and she said it was the first time anyone had given her anything in her life.

We had another case of an 18-year-old young man who had transitioned out of the system. He came to us a sad young man, having been placed in his short life in somewhere around 10 homes. When we gave him a suitcase, he started crying. He said no one had ever given him anything before. All he'd ever received was trouble and trash bags.

In our organization, we never know what happens to these young people after we give them a suitcase or a backpack filled with essential things they need, but our mission is for the children in the foster care system to feel a sense of hope and self-worth. We want to share the love of Jesus Christ, letting them know that someone cares about them and give them a sense of hope for their future.

ABOUT THE AUTHOR

 Allen McMichael founded Fostering Hope Tennessee, Inc. in 2013 as a Christian-based, family-centered organization with its foundation rooted in Jeremiah 29:11. Fostering Hope Tennessee advocates for the needs of children in foster care, raises awareness through connections with churches and through local community outreach, and provides suitcases, backpacks, and personal care and hygiene items to foster children in the Child Welfare System. One of the organization's goals is to raise awareness to the fact that there are more than 9,000 children in state's custody in Tennessee. Allen is the proud father of three adult children, and grandfather of 12. He and his wife, Sylvia, have been together since August 22, 1958, and make their home in Knoxville, Tennessee. You can find out more about Fostering Hope, Tennessee by visiting the website at: http://fosteringhopetn.com/

CHAPTER 6

Brainstorming for Small Business Success

By: Chris Trezise

I was one of the lucky ones. I knew from the time I was 17 what I wanted to do for my career. By the time I was a senior in high school, I had taken all my mandatory courses which gave me some flexibility in my schedule. That allowed me to take a critical thinking class, which turned out to be an introduction to marketing. We were tasked with developing a product, branding it, and marketing it to our class and professor. I was part of a three-person team and we agreed on a local courier service which would deliver same-day intown packages to businesses. We called our business "Runners," and developed the logo, branded a model vehicle, and even used a music video as a theme song in our presentation, "The Runner" by Manfred Mann's Earth Band. The whole process was the most exciting activity I had ever done in school. To say I was hooked on marketing is an understatement. I knew this was what I wanted to do for the rest of my life.

"Choose a job you love and you'll never work a day in your life." - Confucius

I got my first advertising position before I graduated college. It was for a newspaper advertising network that sold print space across the country to advertisers. My clients ranged from billion-dollar advertising agencies to solopreneurs and everything in between and it was my job to help clients organize their print media buys and work with the newspapers to place their schedules. My position was in sales, but I also got to do a lot of the creative work as well. It was a dream job I enjoyed for many years.

After about 10 years of that job, I started to become dissatisfied with what I was doing and who I was doing it for and prayed asking God for direction in my life. I knew I wanted to do something more, but I didn't know exactly what.

Helping the "Little Guys" Who Need It Most

During my years as a media buyer I saw large corporate advertising agencies spend millions of dollars on marketing with teams of people doing various portions of the projects. I also saw small retailers and business to business (b2b) clients trying to bootstrap their business by doing a lot of the work on their own to compete with their larger competitors. The more I saw the scrappy "little guys," the more I understood where I needed to be. Large advertisers with in-house teams and big advertising agencies put budgets together, handle creative design, targeted specific demographics, and marketed to the masses. The small business needed to be a lot more selective and precise. They need the same functions of budgeting, creative design, and demographic research but their targets were a lot smaller. I knew I could help them outsource these functions while maintaining control of their message to their specific target audience and that's how my business began to develop in my mind.

We would think smarter about how to spend money. Looking for low and no cost ways to market, I would introduce my clients to business networking and online marketing. I would find resources that offered quality products at lower costs to my clients. I would suggest ways for vertical marketing to sell more products to the same people and I introduce them to co-op advertising and strategic partnerships.

It was called Brainstorm International.

Passion Killed My Performance and Kick-Started My Company

I let my passion for my new venture cloud my judgement. I allowed my work performance to go way down as I became more and more despondent with my current job. My attitude changed. I no longer enjoyed anything about my current position and in my mind, I created a multitude of reasons why I needed to get out. Although nothing had really changed at work because I was doing the same job with the same people, I saw them differently. It started to show in all areas of my performance and attitude. It's probably at this point where I should have turned in my notice and walked away.

The problem was, I had no formal exit strategy. I just had ideas of what I wanted to do, and they couldn't be implemented at my current employer. I had dreams of what my new organization would be, but nothing written down. I had no one to counsel me. I prayed for answers, but fear clouded my vision and kept me from doing anything about my position. My attitude and performance spiraled downward every day. It just got worse until I was fired.

Truly, I've never once regretted leaving. Where I am and what I'm doing is what I was made to do. How I left fills me with regret all the time.

After leaving my position, I found myself with no job and no ability to support my family. Something needed to be done and done fast. It was finally time for a real plan. I knew what my business was going to do. I'd been developing this idea in my mind for months. While I was not prepared at all for this day, I was ready to face it. My vision to serve small businesses and help them with their marketing was clear.

Learning While Doing

From the start of my business, I knew I had a lot to learn and began looking for development in areas where I was weak. Being in the newspaper business for 10 years working on the creative side, sales side, with advertising budgets, marketing, and more, I was still entering the advertising agency arena with only print media experience in my arsenal. Clearly, I needed additional skills. So, I started working for companies and people that could teach me about other forms of media.

I worked for a printer to understand paper, inks, presses, and plates. I worked for a computer company to understand how computers work, how to get discounts on equipment, and understand networks and how to fix common problems. I interviewed media sales people and production people to get insights into effective advertising and learn the language. I read anything I could get my hands on for product knowledge and how to run a business. I subscribed to peer groups for entrepreneurs and small business owners and took classes about business startups.

I hired my first in-house software engineer to help me develop websites and business software. He was enthusiastic about our partnership and was eager to jump in and work with me. I would do the selling and he would do the development. This was around 1999 - 2000. Websites became part of my agency services because I saw the potential having an online presence would be for companies. Small businesses especially could use a website to level the playing field in many respects because we could make them look just as professional as a large corporate competitor.

Bringing in Staff Before Having a Plan

After that, my first employees came from the University of Tennessee at Knoxville's internship program. Hiring 10 people at one time, they each received college credit from the university and pay from me for their time.

Working inside my home, I gave that multitude of people cubicles, desks, computers, and fancy titles. But I failed to give them training. I had hired so many people at one time, I didn't have the time or the focus to help each one succeed in their position. If they were going to do well, they would have to do it on their own without my help. Some picked up the challenge and ran with it. They were my superstars. They even set the pace for some of the others to follow and made superstars out of them. Others failed to do much at all. They needed my help to succeed, but it was help I was unable to provide or unable to see they needed. Hiring too many people too fast was a waste of precious resources. I was passing out paychecks to everyone. The stress of payroll was a routine that led to many sleepless nights. Looking back, I see now I should have paced my growth.

At the beginning, my attention turned completely to getting the business up and running. I had a whole new "family" of staff relying on me for their livelihood and I'll be honest, it scared the bejeebers out of me. All I could focus on was getting new clients, making sure current clients were happy, and keeping the doors open.

Because the business started in my home, I was there all the time with my real family, but sadly, they became more people I had to deal with. By the way, having 10 employees in your home with cubicles and the works - not a good idea. This just added to the stress on my family, especially my wife, who was externally handling everything pretty well, but internally was an absolute wreck. We all survived, but I will never put that kind of stress on my family again.

The Mistake That Led to a Shocking Financial Discovery

If I was doing it all over, first, I would hire an outsourced CPA to handle my books. Here's why:

When I opened my business, I started with an attorney who proceeded to set up my company as a C-Corp, which I later changed. I also proceeded to hire a person just because they said they knew QuickBooks. This was a bad mistake for more than one reason. First, because I relied completely on this person for a true measure of our financial position, I gave her complete control over the money. I didn't like bookkeeping and was happy to turn it over to someone more qualified, so I thought.

Second, there was no one to confirm our financial position. Whatever my bookkeeper said was taken as fact with no corroborating evidence. After a while, I found out the bookkeeper was not putting any invoices into the system, which made our profits look amazing. The reason she did this was so that the paychecks would not stop flowing, especially hers. I discovered the fraudulent mistakes only when one of my media vendors called and notified me of a $50,000.00 outstanding invoice that needed to be paid immediately or none of my clients' ads would be run. But that was not the only unpaid invoice. All totaled, I owed a little over $100,000.00 and had no reserves to speak of. I was freaking out!

After hearing the news of my horrific financial situation, in a state of shock and disbelief, I left the office and started driving. I had no destination in mind, perhaps Mexico or maybe Kentucky. It didn't matter, I just needed to go. I ended up at a state park somewhere outside of Knoxville. To this day, I have no idea where I was or how I got there. I was in a panic trance. I parked my car and started hiking up a mountain with no sense of what I was doing there.

While hiking to escape my situation or get clarity on it, I can't say, I came upon a clearing which overlooked a mountain vista. There off the path was a worn split log bench rooted on the edge of a cliff. I sat down and started to pray, blaming God (as if it was His fault...). "Lord, I can't believe you got me into this mess, what am I going to do now?" My heavy breathing and panic attack state were slowly subsiding, which allowed me to take notice of the beauty of nature all around me. The view was spectacular. I can still see it in my mind as if it were an unforgettable dream that I keep recalling. The longer I sat the more I prayed for answers. I was waiting for any sign that everything was going to be alright. Alas, there was no epiphany, only the voice in my soul reminding me why I started this business. It became clear the first thing I would need to do is solve the immediate problem. Then I could tackle the next problem and then the next.

Solving One Problem at a Time

I planned to be honest and upfront. I returned to my office in my home still freaking out on the inside, but with a calm resolve on the outside. I contacted vendors and clients and explained the situation. I met with vendors to make payment arrangements and met with clients to ask them to make upfront payments to get their ads placed. I kept this up until everyone was paid.

This may surprise you, but I didn't let the bookkeeper go. I felt that the problem was partly my fault for not being more involved in the numbers of my own business. I did, however, hire a CPA as an outsourced overseer, monitoring everything from then on.

Every book I read before I started my business told me to have clear job descriptions for every position in my company, whether I was doing the job myself or someone else was in the position. This takes time and planning and I didn't know how to do that exactly, which led to hiring everyone with no clear objectives as to what they were to do, no "job duties" and nothing about what was expected of them and their performance. I assumed they would perform their best at whatever they did for me. Yeah right.

After a year of the "ambiguity plan," I had certain sales employees in key roles that had not produced anything in 12 months, not one sale. So, I finally decided to put together a job description along with some expectations and basic accountability. I went over these plans with one employee in sales who had not sold anything since starting. He quit. I laid another person's job description evaluation on my desk and went to lunch. When I returned, she quit. A sick feeling fell over me as I calculated the money and time wasted during that unproductive period. What an idiot I was. My laziness had cost me a lot.

Over the years, my employee count diminished to several outsourced folks that provide services within their specialties. I find this to work best for my business. My outsourced team members have their own businesses and provide expertise in their field. We have systems in place for managing my work and to maintain accountability and performance. I calculate the expenses of each task and the contracted outsourcers agree to our terms.

With Gratitude

I want to thank those that helped me get started. Parker Starr - Radio Group, Evelyn Clark of East Tennessee PBS, The Knoxville News-Sentinel, Danny Butler of Comcast, Eastern Computer, Sir Speedy Printing, Michael Gerber's E-Myth, and I especially want to thank my family for putting up with me through all the turmoil of having an entrepreneur husband and dad. I hope, I pray that I can leave you something that could be considered a legacy. I thank God for allowing me the opportunity to help others through something I thoroughly love doing. I thank God for supplying me and helping me grow every day in my spiritual, personal, and business life.

Get your promised goodies right here:
www.bsimedia.com/bookchapter

ABOUT THE AUTHOR

 Chris Trezise is the Creative Director, Founder, and Chief of Brainstorm International. His strengths are in developing systems and his creativity. Chris is an avid reader and listener to all things marketing and business development. He's a strong advocate for business development groups and collaboration with a passion for helping people grow their business. He loves hearing their stories and helping his customers succeed. He and his wife celebrate 29 years of marriage in November 2018. They have two awesome children, Lauren (27) and Michael (23). Chris and his wife are part of the core at Faith Promise Church where they serve as teachers for the 4- and 5-year olds. Chris continues to learn and grow every day in all areas of life and he feels enthusiastic about the future.

www.bsimedia.com/bookchapter

CHAPTER 7

A Healthy Life with Arbonne International

By: Manuela Scott Ptacek

Growing up with my dad in the Navy, and then marrying a Navy guy, I've moved 16 times all around the world. Knoxville, Tennessee is most certainly my last move, I am now home (or at least I think so!). I once thought of myself primarily as a Californian, however growing up all over the world, I suppose I never really had any specific "roots."

I was influenced greatly by my mom, who was a nurse by education, and who tried to teach us five kids about being more health-conscious well before it was the "in" thing. Though she was normally on the mark, she did mistakenly think that ketchup caused acne and it was banned from our home! And if we had a headache, she would insist we go outside and get some fresh air because that would get rid of it. I dealt with some food and medicine allergies, however I didn't get much information about it at all. I knew that there was a lot of knowledge I was missing, and I did my best to learn (without internet back then) about what I could do to feel better and be better.

I was introduced to my future husband through mutual friends while in college, and working in San Francisco. Eleven months later we were married, and I got to continue the Navy adventure I knew so well from growing up. I enjoyed working for temporary employment services in many of our duty stations so that I didn't have to worry about long-term work commitments. With my husband being a Naval Flight Officer as a Navigator, he was gone a lot, so when he was home I wanted to be home with him. The temporary positions allowed me an opportunity to work for a day, month, or week within various companies. What I enjoyed most about temp work was being able to easily move whenever my husband was working.

Right from the beginning I wanted and valued that flexibility. Being a Navy wife and before that, a Navy daughter (brat), I learned to be flexible in what I wanted to do because of the nature of our life. Flexibility was one of the main things that attracted me to the company I've been working with for years now. With Arbonne International, I own my life.

Entering Health Care – For My Family

Being stationed on several military bases I also enjoyed working in the base hospitals. Being at the military hospitals in several arenas, both as a paid professional and as a volunteer at different times over the years, I was able to connect with many people from various backgrounds. The pediatrics department was my favorite; working with young parents and helping to calm children coming in for various procedures, appointments, and tests was a real joy. It was also there I learned the medical industry is not a health industry; it's a sickness industry.

With much of married life comes kids, we had four. Along with kids comes illness, challenges, and medical issues that we are never prepared for. We had that for sure with each of them.

While doing temporary duty in Japan our first born, Tara, was only five months old and nearly died due to a rare blood infection. Then at two and a half years old, while stationed in Adak, Alaska, the doctors had no idea what was causing new medical issues with Tara so they sent us to a huge Naval hospital in California. Besides night terrors, she also experienced childhood vertigo, and there were other kids on the same island with similar issues. I was beginning to question the environment, the health of the water, air, etc.

If that wasn't enough, when she was close to 13 years old we learned that she had a mild form of Crohn's disease & juvenile rheumatoid arthritis. After years of researching what could have caused her problems, I learned how certain foods and additives could cause joint inflammation, and it was affecting kids in the worst way. (The good news is now Tara is a healthy, feisty young woman!)

Skin Care Without Harmful Chemicals

All my life I struggled with what I thought was extremely sensitive skin; anything I put on my face seemed to make me react negatively. One day back in 2006, I was food shopping and ran into an old friend from our church and she looked gorgeous! I asked her what she was doing because I knew what her skin had looked like before. She said she was using the Arbonne International skin care products and she happily loaned me a package to use for a few days. For the first time in my life I found something my body didn't react to. I was hooked, so that's when I first got involved with the company.

It turns out, my skin was reacting to the many harmful chemicals America allows in our skin care products. Would you put straight bleach on your skin? I would hope not, however, some popular acne skin care lines in America do contain...bleach! Lead is not something most women would want to digest, however, many lipstick brands contain lead as do many brands of mascara you use ladies. And while they think some small amounts are acceptable, no amounts are okay with me!

I finally understood why, during our travels, I was healthier, and my skin was so much better with products overseas. Through Arbonne I discovered the UK and Canada ban well over a thousand more harmful ingredients in personal care products than America does. That's when I knew for sure I wanted to work with Arbonne International as a business.

My Teenager Had a Stroke

However, about a month after I first joined the company our life once again was challenged drastically. Our 15-year-old daughter and third child, Erin, who was a healthy six-foot-tall ice skater, had a stroke. I was shocked because we ate healthy, had our own chickens even, my daughter was healthy and active, and still, she had a stroke. I had to know why, and doctors couldn't tell me.

So, it was back to my research, where I discovered kids *can* have strokes. In fact, our new neurologist told me about her fears that stroke in children would be the next medical epidemic. After her stroke, Erin experienced right-side residual weakness, requiring 19 hours of intense physical therapy. We all were reeling, however, we also felt blessed to have a physical therapist from our church (who could think outside the medical box) take on Erin's case and even started working with her in the hospital for the five days she was there.

On the very same day of Erin's hospital discharge our oldest daughter, Tara, was headed to college for the first time. While I was happy to be taking care of Erin and thrilled she was able to come home from the hospital, the rest of the family took our oldest daughter to college. I missed all the experiences that go with sending off a child into the start of adulthood.

Fast forward several more months: Tara was off at college, my husband, John, and I had an important anniversary, and Erin was recovering. We decided to take our family on our first cruise ever. But then we were hit with another blow of bad health news: the day before we left for the cruise we learned my husband "probably" had "something." The doctor didn't want to spoil the trip for us, so he was vague and gave us a list of four or five possibilities of what it "could be," and cancer was in the mix, but we were told not to worry. When we returned from the trip, he would give us a referral to the doctor he felt would be necessary.

When we returned from the cruise, my husband had a referral appointment at what later turned out to be an oncologist, where he blurted out the word "cancer" for the first time. Even the oncologist was stunned to learn that we had not yet been told it was cancer and told us we looked like "deer in the headlights of a 70-MPH big rig." I guess so.

Turns out John had five inoperable carcinoid tumors on his liver. This doctor also didn't feel radiation or chemotherapy would help. At this point, I was hell bent to figure out what was going on, and why. I started doing research. I wanted to learn why we in the U.S. have higher instances of cancer than in Europe and Canada. The more I learned, the more I understood. I discovered liver and kidney cancers are usually due to outside influences and not necessarily hereditary, like breast cancer can be. And that led me on a search for what could have possibly caused my husband's cancer.

Shampooing His Hair as a Possible Cause for My Husband's Cancer?!

Now, with my degree in business management, I am not the scientific person in our family, that would be my husband, who has a chemistry degree. However, one day after he was diagnosed, John came home from work and saw me in in my office with every product he came in regular contact with laid out on the table. When he learned what I was doing, he started laughing. I was a woman on a mission, determined to find an answer, and so I was googling the ingredients in each product.

About 20 minutes later he wasn't laughing anymore. I discovered the shampoo he had been using every single day for 25 years was not approved for daily use in the United States, even with our low standards, and in fact, this particular shampoo brand had two known carcinogens that were banned in Canada and in the UK. Those two ingredients were cold tar and sodium laurel sulfate. As most people know, our skin is the body's largest organ, but what I learned was alarming: anything touching the skin for 26 seconds or longer will absorb into the skin and can later be found in the body's largest organs. Again, I'm not a doctor, but with my husband using known carcinogens on his scalp every single day for 25 years, with each day being significantly longer than 26 seconds, in a hot shower with pores open, readily absorbing all those dangerous chemicals, well, I thought there might be a connection.

While I searched for an alternative, safe shampoo for my husband (and our whole family), I discovered one important healthy ingredient for scalp issues is Tea Tree Oil. After searching online, I found five different lists of shampoos that met the basic criteria for being healthy and safe. Lo and behold, four of the five lists each included Arbonne's Tea Tree Oil <u>DAILY</u> Shampoo! Although I'd been using Arbonne's skin care products for a while, I didn't even realize the company sold shampoo because when I started, I focused mostly on skin care, which is what Arbonne was known for.

After discovering the Arbonne shampoo that came so highly recommended by various sources online, I had my husband begin to use it and he also began taking Arbonne's men's vitamins I had just learned about.

We Stopped "Feeding" the Cancer

With the kind of cancer John had, the only "treatment" prescribed at that time was to give him a statin shot to help reduce the physical effects. He was told to go for regular scans every six months to see how fast this thankfully slow-growing cancer was progressing.

Six months after his diagnosis and having made those two changes in the shampoo and vitamins, John had his next scan. We followed up with the doctor who said, "Well, looking good," and didn't say anything much more than that. Six months later, following the same daily use of safe shampoo and healthy vitamins, the doctor looked again and said, "Hmmmm..." with no further details. Another six months passed, still continuing on with the healthy changes, and after the next scan, perplexed, the doctor said, "Now, wait a minute. What are you guys doing?! Because this cancer hasn't grown at all!" That's when we knew we'd hit upon something with the two simple changes we made. I told the doctor I firmly believed we stopped "feeding" the cancer with chemicals that were primarily coming from his shampoo.

My husband has continued using the safer shampoo & taking the vitamins, and now for six years, according to his medical doctors, we successfully stopped the advancement of this cancer, which was not able to be medically treated in any way, and normally would have grown a fair amount during that time. The doctors don't call it remission, because he's not cured of the cancer, and he still gets the statin shot once a month for the cancer's side effects, but they have gradually spaced out his scans to once every two and a half years now. We call that miraculous progress.

Because of my husband's diagnosis, we have been even more cognizant over the years of what ingredients are in the products we use, what we bring into our home, and super vigilant about what we allow into our bodies. One of the things I love about Arbonne is the company uses the UK and Canadian standards for personal products ingredients, which are stricter and more stringent than US standards. Shockingly, the US bans only 11 ingredients (see source: https://www.fda.gov/cosmetics/guidanceregulation/lawsregul ations/ucm127406.htm), while Canada and the UK ban 1,733 ingredients in personal care products (sources: https://eur-lex.europa.eu/LexUriServ/LexUriServ.do?uri=OJ: L:2009:342:0059:0209:EN:PDF and https://www.canada.ca/ en/health-canada/services/consumer-product-safety/ cosmetics/cosmetic-ingredient-hotlist-prohibited-restricted-ingredients/hotlist.html).

This year, 2018, Arbonne announced they are exceeding even those standards by banning 2,000 ingredients in our personal care product line.

Other things that make me proud of working with Arbonne is the company is botanically-based, certified gluten-free, certified cruelty-free, and certified vegan. The company doesn't test on animals or use animal byproducts, so they are hyper-focused on making sure what goes into and on people's bodies is safe for everyone.

Freedom, Flexibility, and Financial Fabulousness

After a lifetime of needing flexibility, and living the military life, I am so grateful to have found Arbonne. Men and women of all ages can do this business. If you're coachable, you can take this business wherever you want. I wish I had known about it when I was traveling around the world because Arbonne operates in many countries including Poland, Australia, New Zealand, Taiwan, Canada, the United Kingdom, and is based in the United States.

It's amazing the wonderful feeling of freedom having control over my own life. There's no glass ceiling. I call my own shots and people can make as much money as they want/need to make. And the nice thing is that when life throws you curveballs (and don't I know about those!) you can still have income coming in with the residual aspect of how the company works. In fact, Arbonne's residual income is WILLABLE, so if anything happens to me, my residual income and commissions will continue and go into an estate for my family. Now that is peace of mind!

Everyone in my family is doing well now, thanks to everything we learned and the healthy changes we made. One of the first things I ask people who have been going through cancer is, "What have you changed since being diagnosed?" They usually talk about getting better rest and better foods, however never do I hear about them changing the products in their shower!

We must educate ourselves and break that habit of "I've used that for years" and begin to see that the products people have used for years could be the cause or catalyst for cancer or other health issues. Arbonne can help! I love this company, I love how I have grown, and I love representing them!

Be blessed!

ABOUT THE AUTHOR

 Manuela Scott Ptacek is an Independent Consultant with Arbonne International, and fierce advocate for education in health and wellness. Proud (now retired) Navy wife and Navy daughter, she actively supports our military members in uniform. She possesses the highest love of our country, because she knows what freedoms other people will never see in too many foreign countries.

Manuela has received several awards for her humanitarian efforts. Now, after homeschooling her four (now grown) children for 22 years, she enjoys singing bass with her K-Town barbershop chorus, volunteering activities with her Catholic church, being on crews for hot air balloons, modern square dancing with her husband, John of 37 years, camping with their trailer or simple travelling adventures together... just not moving ever again!

If you would like to learn more about Arbonne, contact Manuela at www.mptacek.arbonne.com
865-227-6825
Facebook: Manuela Ptacek, Arbonne Independent Consultant
Instagram: manuela_with_arbonne

CHAPTER 8

Mentorship Makes All the Difference

By: Mark Field

I remember how excited I was to be attending college at the University of Tennessee, but a year or so after starting my college career, my parents went through a difficult divorce. Because of the divorce, my father was unable to continue paying for my college while supporting two households financially and pay child support for my younger sister still at home. After leaving school, I went to work full time for a few years where I was making just enough money for a single guy to get by. However, eventually I realized if I was going to find a professional career I would need to go back and get a degree.

By that time, I had married my wonderful wife and I was working in retail at a men's clothing store. With my wife's encouragement and the flexible schedule that retail work afforded me, I decided to go back to college. This time I attended Tusculum College, which is now Tusculum University, through their adult learning degree program.

I'll never forget what happened one afternoon about a semester or so away from completing my degree. While taking classes at school and working full-time at the store, I had become the assistant manager of the store. That day a gentleman came into my store and told me he had done business with me quite a few times. He said he was very impressed, and wondered why I was working in a retail environment and had not entered some sort of a professional sales career or done something that was more in line with what he felt my talents and abilities were suited for. I explained to him the truth: I'd gotten stuck, lost my self-confidence, hadn't been ready for greater responsibility, and felt badly about not finishing my degree sooner. Certainly, until I finally completed my degree, I wasn't going to apply for jobs that required one. What he said next astonished and excited me. "If you will finish your degree and come see me, I will make it my mission to get you a job in professional medical sales. I'll do everything I can to help you."

"Making It A Mission to Get You A Job"

That man's name was Chuck Naill and the providential meeting that day made a profound impact on the rest of my life. Chuck only knew me in the environment of being an assistant manager in a men's clothing shop, yet he was willing to stick out his neck and mentor me. He cared about me - not out of necessity, or because we were family, or out of any sense of obligation; he simply wanted to help me as my mentor. I honestly don't know his exact motivation other than he was an answer to prayers, but that conversation encouraged me to accelerate my goals.

Of course, I called Chuck after I finished my final semester. We met for lunch and he was every bit as encouraging then as he was when he first made me the promise to find me a job in medical sales. He explained what the job entailed, what responsibilities I'd have, and he asked me if I was up for it. I felt like I had finally matured enough professionally and would be fully capable of doing what he described, so I agreed. He proposed we make a pact, saying, "If I go out there and find you a job, will you work hard at it and be committed to it?" I was more than willing.

Within days, he landed me an interview with a company in the home health care business out of Louisville, Kentucky called Rescare. I was hired, and my first job was calling on physicians and asking them to refer patients to our home health care services.

Givers Gain

Once again, I had the opportunity to be mentored. This time it was by three leaders at that company: Karen Brown, Pat Phillips, and Janet Gatton. Those women were incredible mentors, pouring in a lot of effort, time, and patience to make sure I was successful. I'll be forever grateful for them embracing me almost as a family member and helping me succeed.

Because of what Karen, Pat, and Janet taught me about the mindset of "Givers Gain," I never went into a physician's office to do my sales job without some sort of an academic whitepaper or a magazine article or something I had learned which would have been beneficial to that physician or his support network around him. I didn't walk in there saying, "Hey, you need to give me business because we're a great company." I would go in and focus on being a trusted adviser, sharing some new treatment modalities I'd discovered or some new regimens for them to consider for helping their patients get back on their feet quicker. I would always go in with helpful tools and resources to offer them. That "Givers Gain" mentality of trying to help people first and then allowing them to help in turn has certainly worked for me all these years.

After a while, TennCare was coming in to Tennessee, which was a managed care option for indigent folks and people who are on Medicaid, but we didn't have anybody in our company who understood the TennCare program, or even managed care for that matter. So, my boss suggested I learn about managed care and insurance to be able to help the company as the changes in the laws and options would surely impact our company in the not-so-distant future.

I used the University of Tennessee Library, this time on weekends and evenings, where I researched managed care, the commercial insurance marketplace for medical care, and more. Before long, I had become one of our company's experts, especially for managed care and insurance in Tennessee. This led to a promotion to director, with a proverbial bigger seat at the table and more influence in the decisions my company was making in our market.

Eventually the senior vice president of Rescare went on to become the president of the largest home health care company in the nation at the time called Olston Health Management and he hired me to be a regional vice president. While I experienced some good fortune, I was a road warrior on that job, except I didn't enjoy the travel at all. I hated being away from my family and being away from home.

In looking locally for opportunities for work that didn't require travel, I found a position in a managed healthcare network in Knoxville, where I live. Once again, in this new company I had great mentors in Lisa Wear, our President at the Initial Group, Dale Collins, the CEO of Baptist Health System, and Rich Williams, the CEO at St. Mary's Health System, which were the owners of the managed healthcare network. There was also a young man named Steve Clapp who worked as the director of network development at Baptist, who I also considered a mentor. All these fine people had years of experience in healthcare and I am grateful for what I learned from them.

Time to Pay It Forward

As part of the work I did for that company, I was invited to join the board of directors of the Knoxville Chamber of Commerce and became the head of the marketing committee. Because of my position at the chamber, I knew they were looking for a director or vice president of membership at around the same time I discovered the company I was working for was looking to sell the Initial Group, so I decided to throw my hat in the ring for the position at the chamber and got the job.

With four people in that position within the most recent five years, there was heavy turnover and the leadership hired me to create a turnaround, not just in the position, but with all the membership efforts.

When I arrived at the chamber in 2004, we had about 1,575 members and a retention rate at right around 76%. Now, in 2018, we have more than 2,300 members and a retention rate of about 89%. For me, it has been a good opportunity with a lot of room for growth because I had a chance to do what I love to do - coach people.

As you can see, I've been mentored so generously throughout my career by people who didn't necessarily have to but took me under their wing anyway.

It may sound like a cliché, but I stand on the shoulders of some consummate professionals who put a lot of time and effort into my career, groomed me, and cultivated me. They recognized leadership abilities in me at a time I didn't even recognize myself. I am forever grateful to them for helping me gain self-confidence and a positive self-image as a professional. From modeling business decorum to understanding how to manage myself in meetings and how to be persuasive without being pushy and how to interact with people from all different backgrounds.

Following these same principles, I went from dealing with people who were mainly heads of manufacturing companies to the chamber with a whole new level of dealing with business owners in the community who don't have a lot of time. My job became communicating effectively with them to find out how the chamber could become a good resource for their needs. If I look for ways to help others, my work is always gratifying, and it's easy to be successful.

Arriving at the Knoxville Chamber of Commerce as the vice president of membership in 2004 with four employees reporting to me gave me the chance to pay it forward, and that became my mission as I built a team. Focusing on helping my team members develop and providing them the same lessons I'd been taught over the years along with their hard work and dedication, culminated in us being recognized as one of the top chambers in the country. In 2011, we were named National Chamber the Year by the American Chamber of Commerce Executives. I now have 13 employees reporting to me in the areas of membership, sales, retention, marketing, and events.

Open Your Heart and Mind to People Around You

My whole career has been built on networking, meeting good people, and having a Giver's Gain mentality of trying to help others before I ask them to help me. Again, one of the lessons I learned from my incredible mentors was if you become a trusted adviser to someone else and are willing to help them, they will then happily will return the favor - not out of a sense of obligation, but because they want to help you like you helped them.

In addition to my work, I am also an active participant in civic organizations like the Mental Health Association of East Tennessee, Legacy Parks Foundation, and sit on the Tusculum University Advisory Board. So, here's a guy that didn't finish college on time and now is on a college president's advisory board.

Many people figure out what they want in their 20s, get married, settle into their careers, and get on with life. But for me, I was immature for a long time. Back in college I had a hard time dealing with my parents' divorce and made some poor decisions based on my immaturity. I thought I would take a year or two off from school to save money and get right back to it, but the part-time work became full-time work. Again, in my immaturity, I was okay with just getting by. I didn't marry my wife until I was 32 years old and mature enough to handle the responsibility of being married. Finally, I matured spiritually and became a Christian around age 34. All this as my professional career matured as well.

Understand Givers Gain. Don't be afraid to listen to other people and build networks and communities of trusted advisers. Look for people you open your heart to, are transparent with, and that you can take constructive criticism from without fear of retribution. Be mature enough to take that constructive criticism and use it to advance yourself as opposed to being defensive and negative. All my mentors over the years could be hard on me, but it was focused and channeled in a productive way, so I could learn from it. I never felt like anyone was being unfair to me.

Today I am blessed to work with a nationally recognized team and to give them the support, resources, tools, and most importantly the mentoring they so richly deserved that I also have been given all these years.

ABOUT THE AUTHOR

Since January 2004, Certified Chamber Executive Mark Field has been responsible for increasing the membership at the Knoxville Chamber of Commerce. Now the Senior Vice President of Chamber Development, he oversees various departments including: membership, events, marketing and communications, public policy, and project management. He is active in the community, serving on the board of directors for organizations such as the Legacy Parks Foundation, Innovation Valley Health Information Network, Community Health Council, and the Mental Health Association of East Tennessee. He also sits on the state advisory board for Tennessee Small Business Development and is a member of the Tusculum College President's Advisory Council. Married to Vickie, Mark has two step children, seven grandchildren, and one great grandchild. He makes his home in Knoxville, Tennessee.

Mark Field, Senior VP of Chamber Development
Knoxville Chamber, 5-Star Accredited Chamber
17 Market Square, #201, Knoxville, Tennessee 37902
865-246-2607
mfield57@att.net
Twitter: Field101
Instagram: Mfield57

CHAPTER 9

It's Never Too Late to Live Your Dream

By: Jim Johnson

Before I start my story, I'd like to thank the Lord, for without Him none of this would have been possible. I also thank my awesome wife, Wendy, who has stood beside me over the last 30 years through the good times and the hard times and has always believed in me. I love you, honey. Then there's my awesome mom and dad. My dad was the most committed worker I've ever seen. He never called in sick, and never missed a day, until he was exposed to ammonia gas, which almost took his life. His dedication to his job taught me to give it all I have. Nothing happens unless you show up. I remember mom always showing me in life that I could do anything I put my mind to and don't let anyone tell me otherwise. She took on challenge after challenge in her life by pushing through the things in front of her and never quitting until they were complete.

During the 1980s my mom set me on the path that lead me where I am today. When I was 14 years old she bought the family a video camera and that's when it started. My mind began working and thinking about all the possibilities. I was like a rock star with that camera. My buddies and I would go into grocery stores and interview people doing taste tests like we saw on TV. You know the ones where they put Coke against Pepsi or Skippy peanut butter against Jif. That was fun until we got kicked out of the store! The manager came along and said, "You can't do that. You're bothering people in here." So, I asked, "Well, can I do it outside?" Surprisingly, they let me set up a table outside the store. I think it was at that point I really got bit by the video-making bug. It was so cool, interviewing people and later making music videos with my little brother, Steve, and my friends. I loved it.

As I got older I got into BMX racing and freestyling. I was so enamored by it, and I wanted to be one of the best in the BMX racing world. After three years of trials, tribulations and wiping out more times than I can remember, I got my shot. At age 16 I qualified to race at the national championships. When the gate dropped I kept saying to myself, "GOOOOOOOOO!!!!!" I wanted it more than anything in my young life. As I listened to "Eye of the Tiger" repeatedly on my Sony Walkman, I kept saying to myself, "I'm going to win this thing!" After qualifying, I ran the final race like I was on fire. I heard people screaming something but I couldn't understand because I was so focused on the race. When I crossed the finish line first, the crowd erupted like a movie! I did it, I won the national championship. In my cloud of excitement, I reached back to grab my seat, only to discover it broke off in the first turn. What people were screaming was, "Don't sit down!" True to life: if you want something bad enough you don't have time to sit down. Although I loved racing, at the heart of why I did it was to make my dad proud of me.

I moved to Knoxville, where I went to Tennessee Institute of Electronics to start a life in the electronic world. I finally earned my associate degree in electronic technology but as soon as I graduated I received the paperwork to be sent to Desert Storm as part of the US Army 844th Combat Engineering Battalion. My time in Iraq was spent driving trucks and bulldozers with my M60. I fully intended to go back to school. However, being in a war has a way of changing a person's mindset, so when I got back home sitting back in a classroom wasn't going to be for me. I knew there had to be something I could do.

Beginning a Life of Entrepreneurship

Upon returning home from Desert Storm at age 24, I had a friend who said that he had a new idea for a business cleaning awnings and wanted me to be his partner. He said, "There are awnings all over the place. I'm sure we can make money!" I didn't have any other plans at the time. Video was just a hobby I had as a kid and wasn't on my radar at all.

So, in 1991, we started the awning business, but about a year into it, we weren't making much money. That's when I suggested we go to Florida because the weather there is good all year round and I was sure we could get even more business accounts. I also had a sister there who I had never met, which was the main reason I wanted to go there specifically. We only had a couple hundred bucks, so if we went, we would have to force ourselves to knock on doors to sell jobs to make money to get back home, or beg on the corner for gas money to get back.

We went, I met my awesome sister, and I'm not going to make the work sound easy, because it was tough knocking on doors, but by doing this we got one of our biggest clients – a very large restaurant franchise. We had doors slammed in our faces so many times I lost count, but we kept at it. Sometimes all it takes is 20 seconds of courage. One day, we went into a large restaurant chain location in Tampa and cleaned and gloss-sealed an 8-foot-by-8-foot section of awning so the managers could see the difference. They saw a difference all right, and that was the beginning of a years-long business relationship. Soon, we were cleaning all locations of this restaurant chain across the east coast from Michigan to Miami. Our business grew substantially, which called for more time on the road. Business was great, but it was hard on my family. I had to make a change.

Raising a Family and Surrendering to God

I really missed my family. I felt like being on the road when I had young children at home was not a good plan. I didn't want to miss my kids growing up. So, I left the awning and pressure washing business and took a job working for Steinberg's as a salesman. Within two years I had become a senior manager and took one of the worst producing stores and turned it into their highest gross profit margin store. After several years there, I was on top of the world. Then one day, I felt like God was telling me to quit. I remember thinking, "I'm sorry, God... I'm not sure that's you. We took this store and turned it around; they're loving me and now why am I supposed to quit?!" After two months of what I felt was serious oppression coming from God, I surrendered.

"Okay God, I just know it's gotta be you telling me I have to leave. I don't even know what I'm going to do." But I left anyway. A month later I received my final check and the very next week the company filed bankruptcy and went out of business. It was so crazy! I thought, "Okay God, I'm going to do a better job of listening to you in the future!"

After I left Steinberg's, I went back to my awning business because the kids were older. It was time to get serious about growing this business, so my brother Steve partnered with us. We couldn't have done it without him. Steve is one of the hardest working guys I know when there's a job to be completed. With him on board we continued to grow over the next three years. Things were awesome. But as you know, times change, sometimes quickly. Without warning one of our biggest customers started closing stores. My friend and my brother went on to continue the awning business and I moved on to what was one of the most fun things I've ever done in my life.

Two of my buddies called me with a crazy idea. They purchased a classic car parts warehouse with over half a million parts from a guy who had been collecting them for 35 years. They asked me if I wanted to work with them selling car parts on eBay. It sounded like fun. It felt like Christmas every day, finding classic parts tucked away in a box never knowing what we might find. We had a blast and we soon became the largest dealer of classic car parts in the United States, and we also shipped car parts all over the world. Things were going well for about three and a half years until the tsunami hit Japan and Hurricane Katrina hit

New Orleans. Gas prices went through the roof, times were uncertain, and people stopped buying classic car parts on eBay. It was hard on everyone at that time.

Remembering Video While at a Crossroads

With the ending of the car parts sales business, I was at a crossroads. I'd always heard the saying, "If money didn't matter and you could do anything in your life, what would it be?" Being a race car driver was the first thing that sprang to my mind, but as I started to think about it, I remembered how much I enjoyed making videos as a kid. It was so much fun for me and the more I thought about it, the more I thought making videos could be an amazing career.

So, I went to the local video production company where the owner of the company was a friend of mine, and I asked him if I could answer the phones. He agreed, and I figured I would only be there for a few months, but I fell in love with it. After a few weeks, I said, "I'm interested in doing more than just answering your phone and you don't have to pay me more until I have mastered it." Again, he agreed, and I learned the video business from the ground up: lighting, equipment, audio, all of it. I worked there for seven years until I was ready to go out on my own.

Over the years, I've done music videos, corporate videos, movies, DVDs, documentaries, news, famous talk shows, and live broadcasts as well. I have also worked on Dolly Parton productions, Netflix documentaries, and all sorts of video shoots.

My first big gig was an episode of "America's Most Wanted." I selected a team of video people and took them to Alabama where we were part of a police sting operation. This guy was attacking women who were selling their wedding dresses. He'd done this in different places in the country like California and Colorado, but the case went cold for about six months until a detective's wife listed her wedding dress for sale. The guy called her, and she realized the questions he

was asking were weird, so she told her husband, the detective, and the cold case got flaming hot again. "America's Most Wanted" got involved and they called us.

We were a production contractor. When something happens in the southeast, national shows call a production company to hire a crew to cover the story. Normally they give us the parameters of the story and some of the shots they want. This one was very different. This was no re-enactment. This was no re-enactment. It was real life, happening in real time.

The attacker called from a different payphone than the two we were set up at and we were racing through town, jumping out of the cars with cameras rolling. We caught the man on camera as the police apprehended him. It was surreal to see this thing play out the way it did with so many people behind the scenes to catch this horrible person. To this day, 13 years later, I'm still friends with the lead detective on that case. I even shot his daughter's beautiful wedding a few years ago.

Response-Ability and Relationships

We all have a responsibility and we all have abilities. How we respond to that ability is on us. I was reluctant to even mention this story, but I think it is important to share. Not for me, but for the man I talked to. A few weeks ago, after a video shoot in Nashville, I was on Broadway, one of the busiest streets in town, where all the tourists go. Homeless people with signs were everywhere, yet nobody was paying attention to them. Nobody. So, I went to my car and grabbed some cash and gave some to each homeless person I saw. I still didn't feel like I was doing anything. That's when one man stood out more than the rest.

He looked to be in his 70s and was sitting with his dog who looked like Toto from the "Wizard of Oz." I didn't care what anyone else thought, I sat with him right there on the sidewalk for almost an hour. He had one heck of a story from his teen years as a Vietnam veteran and the trials and tribulations of the last 50 years of his life. What a meaningful conversation we had! That's what I mean about responsibility. I had the ability to take some time out of my day to sit and talk with someone that needed to be seen and heard. At any moment in life, any one of us could be a decision or two away from putting us in the same position, myself included.

The Start of Something Life-Changing

While developing my video career, my best friend, Rob Brown, and his wonderful wife, Francie, along with myself and Wendy started a non-profit organization called Gen 225 with our vision being everyone engaging their story and boldly leading their friends and family. The mission is to lead people to experience God in the story of their past, present, and future. Rob and Francie have dedicated their lives to the organization full time; I've never met anyone with more compassion for people. I believe everybody wants to have authentic relationships with others, however, we all have baggage we don't want people to know about. I know the devil uses our past against us, but if we can be transparent with our friends then he will have nothing to use on us. At the non-profit they hold retreats where people can authentic, tell their stories, and talk about the worst parts of their lives without being judged. We all have something we've done or have had done to us that we are ashamed of, but when we share those stories in a safe place without judgement, we learn that burdens shared lightens your load.

Since then Rob and Francie have developed and delivered more than 100 retreats with more than 1,000 people in 18 states and Canada, for men, women and couples. My life today wouldn't be the same without having gone through this incredible journey, and I am humbled to have been a part of that experience. To find out more about this ministry visit www.ClickToLookInside.com.

It's been a wild ride so far, and I even left out a few things! If you would like to hear more of the story, let's set up a one-to-one meeting. I'd love to hear your story as well. Doing a lot is just my way.

In fact, for years I'd be working until 3-4 AM every night and needed to do something to be able to focus. My doctor suggested various popular chemical cocktails, but one made me a lunatic and the other made me an emotional wreck. We found still another I could tolerate, but after several years of that my blood pressure was high and my anxiety levels were off the charts. Three years ago, I found a product by Nerium (yes, that's another thing I do in all my spare time!). The product is EHT created by Dr. Stock of Princeton University and his son, Dr. Stock of Signum Biosciences. By taking EHT I can complete my projects without losing focus. I'm better today than I've ever been. Looking younger, feeling younger, and thinking better. Visit www.BabyfaceJ.Nerium.com to find out more about these incredible natural botanical products and how they are changing lives all over the world.

I learned a long time ago connections and relationships are the key to moving forward. Most of this story would not have been written if not for networking and the relationships. Get involved with your Local Networking Today International group. If there's not one in your area go to www.NetworkingTodayIntl.com and start one. Get out of your comfort zone, get out and network. You never know who your next contact will be and how they could affect your life or even better how you could affect theirs. Be blessed and remember to keep on being a blessing to others.

ABOUT THE AUTHOR

 Jim Johnson runs a video production company in Knoxville, Tennessee, and is also a senior director for Nerium International, one of the fastest growing anti-aging companies in history. He enjoys spending time with his wife, their adult children, and 5 grandchildren and recently decided to be a show host of his own video talk show about the Smoky Mountains called, "Smoky Mountain Neighborhood," which you can find on YouTube. Jim has also started a show with his wife, Wendy, and close friends, Darryl and Renee Mackley (owners of Mackley Jewelers in Knoxville), on weekend RV trips around the southeast showcasing camping life and the people who they meet. Be sure to check out, like, and share their Facebook page, "Living Life RV Style." It's all about getting and giving the most in life. You can contact Jim via email at ALifeofQuality.Jim@gmail.com.

CHAPTER 10

Lessons Learned in Opening My Chiropractic Practice

By: Dr. Shana Sparks

People always ask, "Why did you want to become a Chiropractor?" Of course, I have an answer for that. I wanted to help people naturally get better using Chiropractic, without the use of drugs or surgery. When people ask, "'How did you get started?" I have a story to tell. My beginnings were not always pretty or perfect, but there is a reason WHY I decided to begin.

Going into business, I dreamed of the end result: being established and well-known in my community. I have dreamt of busloads of people walking into my office, laying on my adjusting tables, performing a life-changing chiropractic adjustment to the patient, and them miraculously getting up off the table smiling! I have dreamt of the patients loving me and my practice, and then referring all their friends and family to me! I dreamed of my new car, a big house, having kids, taking vacations and early retirement! I dreamed of having "the good life," what I think of as "the American dream."

What they don't tell you is that your dream is going to require WORK, one of the most hated four-letter words in the English dictionary, along with TIME. These are the things you are going to need for your dreams to come true and be successful. Work can look like many things: sweat equity, worry, anxiety, fear, or working by yourself. I learned a lot of lessons along the way, and this is my story.

Lessons Learned about The Good, The Bad, and The Ugly

Prior to marrying my husband, working as an associate doctor, I had the opportunity to learn what <u>not</u> to do in business. Working for someone else and following their rules as an associate for five years, I decided what I liked and didn't like about the way they ran their business. During this time, while my now-husband was in Afghanistan fighting for our freedoms, I myself was living daily with the fear of losing my job after near daily threats, anxiety of saying or doing the wrong thing, and worries about being lied about to others.

During this time, I learned some good lessons, gained valuable customer service experience, learned how to adapt to people's personalities, and how to sell life-changing Chiropractic care. I saw hundreds of people a DAY, adjusting them by hand, and somehow connecting with each one of them. I learned to treat people how I want to be treated, do what I promise, and ask lots of questions. The bad and the ugly included being in a practice filled with lies, bankruptcy, insurance fraud, and deceit. During this challenging time, I was verbally and mentally abused, and led to believe I had to question everything I did in Chiropractic.

After getting married, much as I wasn't ready to leave Knoxville, my husband got orders to be stationed in coastal Georgia, and so we went. After leaving Tennessee and awaiting approval to get my chiropractic license in Georgia, I got a job as a bookkeeper and cashier at a local supermarket. At home I had become successful at lining someone else's pockets while living in fear, worry and constant anxiety. Now, in a new city and state, I was upset having left my friends behind, my Knoxville behind, and I felt alone. In those short few weeks, I was reminded of why I became a Chiropractor in the first place. I love being around and helping heal people.

Personal injury Chiropractic has always interested me and at this time, I was willing and ready to gain the experience. Within a month, I drove to Atlanta to meet with a personal injury Chiropractic firm in town and convinced them to hire me and replace the current doctor. I assured them that I could do better than the current doctor, incentivize people in the local community to come in, and process each personal injury claimant faster.

After three years in Georgia, my husband got out of the Army, moved back to our beloved Knoxville, and found a job, so, I put in my notice to leave the personal injury firm. Although they asked me to stay another year, I declined because I knew it was time to make my own rules. I wanted to be the boss, call all the shots, and have weekends and holidays off.

Lessons Learned about Banks, Families, and Loans, Oh My

When I began my own chiropractic practice in north Knoxville, other than knowing I wanted to go into practice for myself, I was not sure exactly where to start. First, my husband and I gathered lots of data, then sat down with the Small Business Admin and wrote an airtight, fail-proof business plan. We took that plan to bank after bank asking for a loan to start and open a practice.

At one bank, the banker listened as I passionately told my story of seeing hundreds of patients a day as an associate doctor, then working at a personal injury firm, and upholding my Army wife duties. I was elated he agreed with me, gave me hope, and told us he would look over our business plan and give us a call. Unfortunately, he never returned my calls and eventually told us that we needed at least $100,000 of collateral to secure our loan request of $125,000. The lesson I learned: Even though the bank denies you that does not mean it's over.

Here's what plan B looked like: I had a knowledgeable, business-minded, and wildly successful family member look over our plan. We consulted with them for advice, what to do, and where to go next. I came up with a binding agreement for a personal loan and asked them to buy into us. With my hopes and dreams on the line, I asked for $10,000 to get started, which would give me the bare bones I needed to begin. In my naiveté, I presumed family sticks together and this relative would help me out. However, they told me no.

Shocked, disappointed, and afraid my dreams were never going to come true, I kept pressing forward. Being married to a military man, I learned that we do not retreat, only fall back and regroup. After regrouping, we moved on to Plan C and thought to ourselves, "Let's ask ten people for $1,000 each to get our bare bones operation going. Surely, we know enough successful people to take a chance with a $1,000 versus $10,000, right?!" Wrong! We found out who our friends were, who really believed in us, and from the rest heard all the excuses of those who "wish they could" help us.

Lesson Learned: Three Strikes Doesn't Mean You're Out

After much discussion, we found an arrangement that might work to get my foot back into the community. I decided to independent contract out of a space with people who offered to be a "stepping stone" to help me out. This sounded promising and my hopes were renewed. I was feeling unstoppable and ready to take on Knoxville.

Yet my excitement came to a crashing halt as the front desk assistant told me how deeply nepotistic the office ran. My stomach instantly ached, and a still-small voice told me this was not going to work out. Somewhere in the back of my head I knew that I needed to pack my things and leave. Yet, I thought to myself, "What is the worst that could happen?" After all, I had worked for a man who ran his successful practice into the ground, treating me and his other associates terribly. I questioned if I was even doing the right thing or if somehow, I was being punished for being a bad person. I had been over-worked and underpaid as a Doctor of Chiropractic for several years at this point. I figured, "How bad could this be?" Turns out... worse than I ever imagined; between the nepotism and the family drama playing out around me, with the old familiar lies and insurance fraud it went from bad to worse.

After getting the boot from that office, I found myself lying in bed next to my husband, broke and crying, trying to figure out what to do next. I was at the bottom and not sure if I would ever have my own office. I had failed so many times I began to doubt myself and my abilities. All the feelings of failure started to creep into my mind. I was ashamed, fearful, worried and filled with constant anxiety. My brain got on this merry-go-round of emotion and began to spin. After only a week, I wanted to get off the ride. I was exhausted, but knew I had to get up one more time. I had fallen so many times I felt like the bruises were permanently there.

Amidst the chaos, I had a friend who allowed me to use their space temporarily while I searched for another office. At this point, we had no money to rent, build out, or renovate any office space. We had no collateral to give the bank for a loan. None of our family or friends could help us in any financial way at all. Seems desperate, right? Then I remembered one important detail: I could apply for a small equipment loan from my malpractice company. So, I took a leap off that cliff, asked to borrow $5,000, and held my breath. After everything, I knew the worst they could tell me was no, but instead, they said, "Yes!" I was finally going to be in business for myself!

Lesson Learned: Growing Pains Are Part of God's Plan – and So Are Good People

I knew immediately I wanted to look for office space on Clinton Highway in north Knoxville because that's the area I'd always worked, and I liked it there. I found an office building with small offices to rent and struck a deal with the owner to rent a 200 square foot space with a communal waiting area with chairs. I took the small loan, paid my rent for one year, borrowed a therapy unit from a friend, purchased vinyl banners, and staked them to the ground out front of the building on Clinton Highway. I was in business.

When going into business for yourself another thing people don't tell you about is growing pains. We all know what growing pains feel like when we are little. Our legs may ache and there is not much you can do about it. Growth is painful, but it's necessary. When life in business becomes unmanageable and uncomfortable, I tend to pray away all the discomfort. The reality is, as a business owner I prayed exactly to have all of it. Just like when a patient begins to feel better and life seems to be smooth, but then the headache comes back. There is always that time when an ache or a pain reminds me of my past to get to where we are now. Yet when I am feeling good and things go as I planned, I easily forget all the discomfort and growing pains I had to go through to get here. Sometimes, our plan is not God's plan. Where I am today is evidence to me that God had my back the whole time and He had a way better idea than mine all along.

After practicing in that 200 square foot office with two adjusting tables and one therapy unit, the growing pains began to surge yet again. At this point, I had been in my space for nine months and needed to expand. But to do that, I needed more business and I needed people to know who and where I was. Around the same time, I had seen on Facebook there was a local networking group meeting about two miles from my location. I sent an email, got some info and began to close my one woman show for an hour and a half every Wednesday to attend. Networking Today International was free, meeting once a week, and was nearby; I could not pass up that opportunity. I began to meet local small business owners and workers for other large businesses. Attending every Wednesday for a couple of years, I met some good people, learned about them, and looked for ways I could help them. I started building a strong network of people to bounce ideas off, ask advice, and even occasionally vent to.

With my new and growing network of referrals coming in regularly, I began to frantically search for a new space. A year earlier, I had visited a space in Powell, not too far from my current location. The space had sat empty for two years and I really wanted to rent it. The seven-room space was 2,500 square feet of 15-year-old carpet, a cubicle desk, and a corner vanity fireplace that had never been used. There were hundreds of dead spiders, live spiders, and cobwebs. But all I could see was the potential.

At this point, I had been using Square for my merchant services payment system. I had done enough business with them, that they offered me a $3,000 capital loan - exactly what we needed to rent the office space. What did I have to lose? I applied for the loan, got the $3,000, paid the rent, and began the process of turning on the utilities. I was at square one again, broke, in debt, freaking out, and worried I was going to fail in three months. But I worked hard, tore down walls, removed the vanity fireplace, repainted, retiled, bought computers, and installed an x-ray unit. Today, after four years of being in the same space, we are mostly debt free and continue to improve our processes and patient experiences.

I'd always heard the axiom, "Fall seven times, get up eight." The reality is that if opening a business was easy, anyone could do it. It is much easier to give up and give in than to work for what you really want. Mine is not a rags-to-riches story, no, mine is a story of PERSERVERANCE. I learned to do whatever it takes to make my dreams come true. If I were to offer you advice, I could tell you not to worry about the hardships along the way, but that probably wouldn't stop you from worrying. So, I will say this: Work hard, people will notice, and your efforts will be rewarded. Believe in yourself and LOVE what you do! Breathe and take a step back, you got this. If your story ends like mine, everything IS going to work out and be okay. The final lesson learned:

follow your dream and take a chance. You will probably make it, but even if you don't, you can say you tried!

ABOUT THE AUTHOR

 A native of Augusta, Georgia, Dr. Shana Sparks received her Doctor of Chiropractic at Sherman College of Chiropractic in 2005 and is a licensed chiropractor in the state of Tennessee. She is highly trained in the most recent research and technology of diagnosis and treatment for patients and has been awarded the Service Distinction Award.

Dr. Sparks has practiced in north Knoxville for most of her career where she currently owns and practices at Knoxville Chiropractic Solutions in Powell, Tennessee. She and her husband, Bryan have two English Bulldogs, MooMoo and Scooter.

Contact Dr. Shana at 865-333-0999 for more details.

CHAPTER 11

A Heart for Service and Beyond

By: Matthew Libby

I was born with customer service in my blood. That might be somewhat hyperbolic, but I definitely learned about customer service at an early age. I spent the first ten and a half years of my life living in a country "mom & pop" store and gas station called "The Rose Valley Store" located in Kelso, WA. My family's living room kitchen and bathroom were in the back of the store and our bedrooms were upstairs. I waited on customers as soon as I was tall enough to see over the counter. This was also in the days of full service gas stations, so it was also my job to pump gas, check the customers' oil in their cars, put air in their tires, and wash windshields. It became so engrained in me to say, "Thank you," all the time that to this day I have to make a conscious effort to reply with, "You're welcome," when someone else thanks me!

Outside the store I lived a typical childhood. I participated in Cub Scouts, played little league, climbed trees, and went to Sunday school. When I started school, my elementary school was a separate 1st – 6th grade independent school district. At one time it was 1st – 8th grades. Because each grade only had one class, I went through 1st -6th with roughly the same 30 kids. I rode the bus into town for junior high in seventh through ninth grades and high school was grades 10-12, where I became the commander of my Air Force JROTC, which eventually led to my military career.

During my high school years, I spent several months working at the golden arches where I learned, "If there is time to lean there is time to clean." I had a great experience there and gained some valuable skills, but I wanted more. In the fall of my senior year I was able to secure a position as a bagger at a local supermarket chain called Keil's Park 'N Shop. I stayed there and progressed to working as a cashier after I graduated from high school. If I hadn't enlisted in the U.S. Army I probably would have worked there for many more years.

Active Duty Around the World and a Classroom in Tennessee

Folks are initially confused as to how this country boy from the Pacific Northwest ended up in East Tennessee, but it was thanks to Uncle Sam. Active duty for me commenced on September 27, 1977, at Fort Jackson, South Carolina. After completing my aircraft turbine engine repairer course at Fort Eustis, Virginia, I spent two years in Hanau, Germany. Over the next few years I would have several overseas assignments interspersed with stateside duty in the 101st Airborne (Air Assault) at Fort Campbell, Kentucky, across the border from Clarksville, Tennessee, and I'm still in Tennessee today.

One of the excellent benefits I took advantage of during my 20-year military career was the college tuition assistance.

Taking night courses and CLEP tests I was able to complete my Bachelor of Science degree in Sociology in just 17 years! Upon retirement from active duty, I was able to put my degree to use by becoming a substitute teacher in the Clarksville/Montgomery County Public Schools.

The Perpetual Substitute

Substitute teaching was a great way to supplement part-time jobs or time between jobs as I worked on discovering what my next career would be. I thoroughly enjoyed substituting and worked at all levels from pre-school to high school, and even substituted in the Advanced Placement (AP) classes. The first year after leaving the Army, when I wasn't teaching, I worked a retail job at Radio Shack, and as a car salesman. As I looked for a career instead of another job, I had many prospects that would utilize my education and experience. The drawback was none were local to where I was living. "Must be willing to relocate" was a requirement for every position I wanted. After ending my active duty, I decided I didn't want my employer to dictate where I could live anymore. Even so, I did eventually move, but not for work. Unfortunately, my first marriage had suffered the pitfalls that plague many military couples and we divorced. But the bachelor life was not for me.

In the late 1990s the internet was still in its infancy. I stumbled across a website that connected Christian singles. That was where Janise (my amazing wife of nearly 20 years) and I first got acquainted, so after a few months of long distance dating I relocated from middle Tennessee to east

Tennessee. I again had a short time of unemployment after I moved, and I restarted my search for my post-military career. My substitute teaching experience came in handy as I tried many different occupations with stints of substituting in between. After being on that cycle for about ten years I decided to make teaching a more permanent situation and investigated a couple of two-year programs to attain a teaching degree. At the same time South College was introducing their T.E.A.C.H. program that would award a teaching certificate in one year if you already had a bachelor's degree, which turned out to be the perfect fit for me.

However, although I earned my teaching credentials and completed two teaching assignments over a period of three years, I found myself in the sub cycle yet again. As you can imagine, this over 50-year-old sergeant was not in the highest demand for those Kindergarten through grade six teaching positions that 100s of bright-eyed twenty-somethings with the latest master's in education were clamoring for. Fortunately, I was able to secure a temporary job with my wife's employer which eventually led to a management position in a 24/7 convenience store - back to my grocery store roots!

My Surprise Career – Insurance? Yes!

While I loved the fast pace and friendly exchanges with my regular customers, unfortunately the long hours, and working every holiday and every weekend eventually wore me down. So, I started looking for something that might offer a better work-life balance. That led to a search on the online job boards like Indeed and Monster and that's where I saw an ad about marketing to senior citizens. I thought I clicked on a job listing for a marketing position with an assisted living facility, but it turned out it was marketing final expense life insurance. I decided to apply anyway, got called for an interview, and was able to do a ride-along with the local supervisor. Their methods for developing appointments and sales did not appeal to me at all, but that interview process did kindle an interest in considering an insurance career. My next step was to investigate insurance opportunities as my career.

I never imagined I would get into insurance sales. Fun fact: the guy I had replaced at the convenience store had left to go work in the insurance industry. Maybe it was something in the air there...

Soon I found a company that said they loved to hire veterans, and I submitted my resume. A few days later I had my first interview and was on my way to securing my health insurance and life insurance licenses. I passed both license exams on my first attempt in July of 2013.

I embarked on this new career by marketing voluntary supplemental insurance plans through a business-to-business marketing concept, which required a lot of cold calling on business owners and office managers. While I believed in the quality of the company and the products and services they offered, I just was not able to capitalize on the opportunity. I needed to be able to secure a group of at least three employees to put the benefits in place, however many of the business owners and managers I spoke with were still reeling from the 2008 recession. I would call on businesses that were listed as having 10-15 employees and either find an empty building or an employer saying, "It's just me and one guy left." The other common scenario was, "This Obamacare thing is coming up and until we know what we are doing there we aren't doing anything about insurance."

During this time, I met an agent with my current company. Every other week or so he would contact me about coming to work with him. He would tell me how the opportunity was wide open. As it turned out, he was right. My concerns about being in competition with him if I did switch companies to work with him were unfounded. At the time I didn't realize because I would be working with individuals and not just companies, there was plenty of business to go around. So, I kept putting him off until I heard he was going to open a storefront office in our town. That's when I contacted him and said, "OK if you are opening an office where I can work close to my home I will give your opportunity another look." As I am writing this I am sitting in my second storefront and celebrating my fourth anniversary with that company.

Serving Seniors by Educating Them About Insurance

The individual market turned out to be a much better fit for me. Contacting people who need help because they are confused by the ever-changing healthcare marketplace is much more rewarding to me than knocking on business doors. Even though people have been enrolling in Affordable Care Act plans (ACA) (aka "Obamacare") since 2014, they still find the complicated process understandably confusing. It's my job to keep up with the changes and advise people on their options. The company I work with takes on a three-pronged approach to meeting that necessity. Potential clients come to me with a healthcare need and I embark on a fact-finding process to tailor a plan specifically for them that provides them a wall of protection which includes their major medical coverage, supplemental plans to fill the gaps, and life insurance.

My first few months came during the special enrollment period, so the bulk of my business was getting approved people enrolled in plans they could afford and add a few supplemental and life insurance plans. As we approached the upcoming enrollment season, not only did I need to recertify to offer ACA plans through the Federally Facilitated Marketplace (FFM), better known as the infamous healthcare.gov, but now I needed to certify to offer Medicare plans.

Medicare is a highly regulated market and can be very intimidating when you are new; there's an intensive certification process which must be repeated every year. The first step is to complete national requirements where you only are allowed three attempts to score 90 or above. If you do not pass by your third attempt, you must wait for the next year. After that is completed you must certify with each carrier you wish to represent, and they each have similar qualification requirements.

The self-employed and small employer groups are other aspects of what we offer, but my favorite group to work with is the senior market. If you think the Medicare certification process I mentioned above is confusing to us agents, the individuals that need the plans find them even more confusing. The government has two healthcare programs with similar names, but they are not the same thing at all. Medicare is the program for individuals over age 65 or with certain disabilities while Medicaid is a federal program administered by the states for individuals with low incomes; some people do qualify for both. It is very rewarding when I can help someone discover that they can qualify for additional assistance.

When someone turns 65 they are now eligible to apply for Medicare. When they enroll through Social Security or the Railroad Retirement Board they now have Medicare parts A & B. Medicare A & B covers many medical expenses, but not all. That's where the Medicare Supplement, Medicare Advantage, and Part D prescription drug plans come in – and this is when it gets fun. (Well, it does for me anyway! I love this stuff!) Whenever someone turns 64½ their phone starts ringing, and they get 70 pounds of mail. The exciting part is I get to be a no-cost knowledgeable advisor for my customers. I earn my commission from the insurance carrier when I enroll the new member. That means my customers get my advice and experience for free to them. I sit down with them in their home or my office and review all their options and help them find what fits them.

When people first turn 65 is not the only time Medicare Beneficiaries can select a new plan. Every year from October 15 – December 7 is the Annual Enrollment Period (AEP) for Medicare. The AEP is those dates regardless of what day of the week it is. This is the time anyone who has a Medicare Advantage or Part D PDP can select a new plan for the next year. There are also certain conditions during the year when individuals may enroll or change plans besides the AEP or turning 65. Medicare Supplement enrollees can change plans throughout the year, but their current health can limit their options. As you can see, there are a lot of details, but I enjoy keeping up with the regulations and options, so I can best advise anyone who needs help.

I have always had a desire to serve. Even though I received many benefits for my military time, I was serious and focused on my service. Over the years I've taught Sunday school, sang in church choirs, and have been a church bus driver. For several years I have been the Quartermaster for my Veterans of Foreign Wars post and district. And now I am a busy ambassador for my local chamber of commerce. All of these are positions I signed up for and most have been volunteer positions I have been happy to fill. From the time I was a youngster in my family's store all the way to today, customer service still runs through my veins.

ABOUT THE AUTHOR

Matthew (Matt) Libby is a Licensed Independent Health and Life Insurance Agent in Oak Ridge, Tennessee. He is available for speaking engagements for church groups, senior centers, or civic organizations that serve the senior population to present non-sales, education-only Medicare Educational sessions with no obligation of any kind (in fact, it's a CMS violation to solicit business during a Medicare Educational event). Matt conducts business primarily in Tennessee and Kentucky and holds non-resident licenses for Washington & Oregon. He is happy to answer general questions for people from any state, but legally can only advise in the states where he holds a license. Matt is a 20-year U.S. Army veteran, husband, father, and grandfather.

Contact Info:
Email:MLibby103@gmail.com
Social Networks:
www.facebook.com/AgentMattLibby
https://www.linkedin.com/in/matthew-libby-8912967a

CHAPTER 12

Strategic Leadership with a Mission to Motivate

By: Keith Galloway

I remember the day things changed for me like it was yesterday. I was a high school math teacher and enjoying a day off school for a snow day, happily wasting time just scrolling through Facebook. That's when I noticed an ad for a group called The John Maxwell Team about becoming a professional coach, speaker, and trainer. That really peaked my interest. First off, I LOVE speaking in front of groups. Nothing energizes me more than to share my ideas with like-minded people and inspire them to be better. And second, I respect and admire John Maxwell and his teachings. I was receiving his daily newsletter, and I had read several of his books. So, I clicked on the link and filled out a form to receive more information.

Now if you don't know who John Maxwell is, then I encourage you to look him up. He has authored more than 100 books and trained the governments of more than 100 countries in the art of leadership. He is the definition a "Leadership Guru." He is someone worth following when it comes to leadership development.

I received a call a few days later from a representative of the John Maxwell Team (JMT) to interview me and see if I qualified for the program. At the end of the call, he made an offer for me to join. However, joining the JMT required a significant financial investment. I told him I would pray about it and call back within the next week or two.

I told my wife about the conversation, and how I really wanted to pursue something like this. She was supportive, yet reluctant. Could we really afford it? Did I even have enough time to take this on? We both agreed to pray about it and see where God led us.

Two days later, we went to get our taxes done at H&R Block. Now it is worth mentioning that we usually get a substantial amount of money in our tax return. We put a lot of money aside from our paycheck each month for taxes. Honestly, it's probably not the best way to manage your tax payments, but we enjoy the hefty sum all at once. But as big as our tax return usually was, it would not be enough to cover the John Maxwell Team price. So, when getting our taxes done, we didn't expect much to change.

While in the middle of doing our taxes, the woman assisting us asked about how many children we have. The tax year was 2014, and that is the year my son, Bo, was born. So, with our daughters (Sarah and Reese), that gave us 3 children to claim. Apparently, that third child made a BIG difference in our tax return because it was nearly 70% higher than what we had gotten the previous year. This put the amount of our return about $100 over the cost of JMT. And seeing how my wife and I had been praying about me doing this, it seemed God had given us a clear sign of what we needed to do.

The John Maxwell Team Training

While we had decided that God was pointing us toward pursuing this opportunity, I still had quite a few other responsibilities to think of. First, I have three children that need my attention and guidance. I have my wife, Jennifer who needs my support as well. And then there were my professional responsibilities with Hardin Valley Academy, the public high school where I taught math in Knoxville, Tennessee. As you may imagine, teaching math is a high-pressure position because of the standardized testing and teacher accountability. So, I couldn't cut any corners in the classroom or my students would suffer. In addition, I was the head varsity basketball coach. Add to that, my wife was the girls' head varsity coach as well. I had to handle all of this while taking on the responsibility of training for the John Maxwell Team. I think it goes without saying - we had our work cut out for us.

Without going into a lot of detail about the JMT training, I'll say it requires a significant time commitment. There are two conference calls a week for everyone in JMT, plus an additional small group call that members sign up for with a JMT coach. I also had to lead a group of people in a mastermind, and attend the JMT live event in Orlando. And then I had the online courses I had to take to get the training necessary for each field. While only some of these things were required, I wanted to do everything EXACTLY as they suggested so I would get the most out of my investment. I had no choice but to do all of it.

Honestly, I was okay with everything except for the mastermind. It wasn't that I didn't want to do it. I just didn't know where to find people who would sit through an 8-week mastermind study and I didn't have time to go looking for people. I thought maybe I just shouldn't do it. But was that really giving it everything I had?

As luck would have it, a good friend of mine, Nathan Brooks, owned a company called The Athletic Shop in Chattanooga, where I had grown up. I was talking to him on the phone about needing to do this mastermind group for my training. After talking about what it entailed, he thought it would be good for his management team to go through. So, we set up a time each week to do a one-hour conference call.

Going through the mastermind, I realized that a study on John Maxwell's books wasn't what these people needed. Instead of doing a study, I helped them develop a mission statement. Along the way, we identified some core values for their company, and I helped them solve a few nagging problems. Even though it wasn't exactly what I had planned, it was a productive mastermind, and everyone in the group gave me a lot of positive feedback.

I followed up with Nathan the following week to get some additional feedback. At that point, he asked me if I was interested in being their business coach. Seriously? Business coach? I didn't think I knew anything about business. I've never been in business a day in my life. I was a math teacher and basketball coach. But they weren't looking for a business or industry expert. They wanted someone who knew leadership who could motivate their team in a positive way to develop their teamwork. They wanted someone like me with my experience to coach them through making better decisions. They had seen me in action asking great questions that led to positive outcomes already. And they felt like I was the person who could help them with what they needed. Plus it's always nice when someone says they want to work with you!

As flattering as the offer was, I couldn't do it at the time. Basketball season was coming up, and I didn't have enough time to be consistent with the commitment. However, I agreed to stay in touch and coach them on an "as-needed" basis. In other words, they could call anytime they needed me and I would help if I could.

The 2015-16 Basketball Season

At the beginning of the 2015-16 basketball season, I was excited. My team wasn't very good the year before, but we had a good stretch through our summer camps and had some key players back and we also had some rising talent. Unfortunately though, when you have as many quality players as we had, everyone wants playing time. This caused a lot of tension throughout the season. I think I managed it as well as I could have, but it's difficult for a teenager to understand that being good enough doesn't necessarily guarantee an opportunity to play. For this reason (among others), this season was more stressful than others in the past.

As the season progressed, I began to feel more and more stressed. I had too much on my plate. Coaching high school basketball takes up so much time, and basketball season is about four months long. I got to the point where I didn't enjoy coaching basketball anymore. It was affecting my family life as well. While I was at basketball, I thought about missing time with my family. But when I was with my family, I thought about my responsibilities with basketball. It just wasn't healthy for me to be thinking like that. So, after the season, I had to decide. Should I continue coaching basketball and hope it gets better next year? Or should I stop coaching basketball and take this chance to pursue a new opportunity in business and leadership coaching?

At the end of the season, I decided that the best thing for all involved was for me to resign as basketball coach. However, I wanted to wait until after the end-of-year banquet because the banquet is to honor the players, especially the seniors. I didn't want the banquet to turn into something about me. That night, I had several players and parents come up to me and express their appreciation for everything I had done, which made me seriously reconsider the announcement I was about to make. I truly cared about those kids. I still do. And I love basketball. But I had to do what I felt God was leading me to do. It just wasn't fair to keep coaching when my heart wasn't in it. So, two days later, I resigned from my position as head varsity boys' basketball coach at Hardin

Valley Academy. It was one of the hardest things I've ever had to do.

The Athletic Shop

Since I was no longer going to coach basketball, I could now work with the Athletic Shop. I was still teaching, so my time was restricted from consistently working with them until I could get my schedule worked out properly at school. So, after unofficially working with them for about a year, I became their official business and leadership coach in January of 2017.

That year ended up being a BIG year for The Athletic Shop. They saw growth of nearly 60% in revenue. Their profits almost doubled that year as well. And based on what they were paying me, the return on investment (ROI) was about 2,000%. Not only that, but they moved up to #2 in Adidas team sales nationwide that year (up from #10 two years before). This was a solid list of accomplishments for a first-year business coach's resumé.

I do want to make sure I give credit where credit is due. The Athletic Shop works hard in an extremely tough industry. They are team-oriented, reliable, and customer-focused. Their motto is: "We build meaningful relationships through serving others." They saw a significant ROI in the first year I worked with them, but I give them all the credit because they did the work. As a coach, I'm only as good my clients' actions and results. I am thankful for their work ethic and resilience. The Athletic Shop is full of winners, and that is clear through the results they see. I truly appreciate the opportunity I have to work with them.

From Teacher to Full-time Consultant

As I mentioned before, I was still teaching during 2017 while working with The Athletic Shop. I worked with several clients intermittently throughout that year but didn't get any other recurring clients until the start of 2018. And when summer hit, I decided that I would go all in to try and make this my full-time occupation. On July 15, 2018, after signing a few more clients, I resigned from my position as math teacher at Hardin Valley Academy. The start of the 2018-19 school year marked the first time in 34 years that I did not go back to school in the fall as a teacher or student.

I would be remiss if I did not take this opportunity to thank everyone at Hardin Valley Academy for everything they have done for me and my family. They pushed me every single year to want to be a better leader and a better teacher. In fact, I am certain that I would not have gotten to this point without the support and guidance of the principal, Sallee Reynolds, and her staff. Everyone at that school cares so much about the community and the students. I am grateful for my time there. And while I no longer work there, I am still a Hardin Valley Hawk. My wife is still a teacher and coach there, and my children will go to high school there. It is a fantastic school, and I am so glad to have been a part of everything they are doing.

Being a teacher was tough, but I knew how to do it well. It was ingrained and I had a routine. Entrepreneurship will have a different set of challenges. I understand that. But I don't worry about it because I know I'll make the necessary adjustments and I look forward to the challenge.

What Next?

In going through this transition from employee to entrepreneur, I had to reflect on what I do well and how I can use it to help others. When it comes to my past successes, there is one concept that has never failed me before: SERVE OTHERS BEFORE MYSELF. This is my mission. And I will live up to it.

Here's what I have learned about business leaders: there are three outcomes that all business leaders care about:

1. Making more money
2. Working less time
3. Having less stress

It is my job to help leaders move towards all three of these outcomes. How do I help with this? Honestly, the answer looks different for everyone. But any business leader can achieve them if they are coachable, honest, and resourceful. And for that reason, these are the personality traits I look for in my clients.

I am so thankful for the opportunities that I have been given. I am blessed beyond my wildest dreams, and at the same time I believe this is only the beginning. I know God has great things in store for me and my family. And I am looking forward to the opportunities that this new path will bring.

ABOUT THE AUTHOR

Keith Galloway is a former teacher and athletic coach turned leadership and motivation consultant. As an achiever, Keith has been a 3-sport all-state athlete, collegiate national champion, valedictorian of his class, and championship basketball coach. Keith knows what it takes to compete and lead at the highest levels. While teaching math to high school students since 2004, Keith also began pursuing his passion for lessons in motivational leadership. Now as a business consultant and coach, Keith has earned multiple certifications in coaching and leadership development. In the process, he has helped his clients double their profits, grow their teams, and enjoy more time away from their organizations knowing that company leadership is doing everything necessary to be successful. The father of three children, he and his wife make their home in Knoxville, Tennessee, where Keith still is known to play a game or two of pick-up basketball.

Keith Galloway
Strategic Leadership and Motivation Coach
865-235-1024
keith@keithgalloway.win
www.keithgalloway.win

MORE ABOUT THE CREATOR & EDITOR

From the evening when Felicia attended the Knoxville Chamber of Commerce Schmoozapalooza event which eventually led to the birth of this book!

Felicia Slattery was raised in an unassuming, conservative blue-collar family with a quiet mother who whispered daily to a young Felicia that she could be anything she wanted when she grew up – and she believed it.

As a result, Felicia has led a life of fun, exploration, and excitement, always seeking to learn more about the world. She has spent equal time as a singer in a rock & roll band as she did in a convent – but, of course not at the same time! She's lived and studied in Paris, France, and traveled around northern Europe meeting people from all over the world.

She knows how to say "I love you" in seven languages and loves learning about cultures and civilizations both current and ancient.

As a life-long speaker in front of groups of hundreds, starting at age seven, she has an affinity for the spoken word and can help others to harness their own sometimes jumbled thoughts into a coherent and well-delivered message.

She was ranked on Rate My Professor.com as a "hot" teacher back in the days when she was teaching public speaking and communication courses on college campuses around the Chicagoland area and has held many other jobs in her lifetime including make-up sales rep, pharmacy counter clerk, CD manufacturing rep, babysitter and nanny for children in the US and Paris, waitress, consultant, professional speaker, researcher, author, publisher, and story-teller. But her favorite job is hands-down Mom to her two teenage daughters and wife to her super-hot former football player with an MBA turned personal trainer husband, Brent. They have made their home in beautiful Knoxville, Tennessee since 2015.

Felicia Slattery lives her life with energy, passion and enthusiasm because she realizes each moment is precious. After nearly losing her life during childbirth in 2004, a little more than a year later she began to put her communication and public speaking talents to use to create a positive impact on the world. She has been running her business out of her home while raising her daughters ever since 2006. After being cured miraculously from lung cancer in 2012, her resolve and passion to help people discover and express their God-given gifts only became deeper.

These days Felicia Slattery speaks to group of professionals of all kinds about their communication skills and helps them develop their speaking and business relationship skills. She has shared the stage with notables and best-selling authors like Zig Ziglar, Bob Burg, Michael Port, and Carol Roth and has written and contributed to a number of books, in addition to the four she's written herself. The day she became a #1 best-selling author on Amazon in 2012, she hit her knees and thanked God for allowing her that opportunity.

Her clients have included a best-selling cookbook author from Switzerland; a Harvard-educated Ph.D. freelancer in the Philly area; a couple of celebrities from TV shows you would recognize (and probably watched!); the woman who created the "point to the face to show how you feel / is your pain a 1-10" scale; a dentistry practice with leading technologies; and countless coaches, consultants, authors, and speakers around the world. She's been blessed to have trained and presented to people from some of the biggest Fortune 100 companies in the world.

Felicia Slattery is not only a professional speaker herself but has helped other speakers get booked and make money as speakers themselves to share their own God-given messages with the world.

For fun Felicia sings (tenor!) in the choir at her church in Knoxville (the Cathedral of the Most Sacred Heart of Jesus –

come hear her sing at 9AM Sunday Mass the next time you're in town!), facilitates faith formation classes at her church, volunteers with her daughter's drama club, pulls weeds out of her garden, cooks all her family's meals from scratch (as in she makes her own chili powder and grows many of their veggies and herbs from scratch!), goes to every one of her girls MANY activities from cheerleading to plays to diving competitions, and has acted as an extra in a couple cable TV shows.

You can often find her posting fun and inspirational messages on social media and sharing more tales from her life in written and video form.

More than anything, she is grateful to God for the many countless blessings in her life, counts her work as one of the biggest of all blessings, and looks forward to serving you. You can invite her to speak on your stages and share her stories of overcoming health challenges, life challenges and more to see success while motivating and inspiring others to do the same. Your audiences will feel encouraged, enlightened, and energized after hearing from Felicia.

Contact her at http://FeliciaSlattery.com/contact

If you would like to start your own speaking career visit: http://HowToGetStartedSpeaking.com for a free gift to help you get started.

To have your story appear in an upcoming edition of *How Did You Get Started*, contact Felicia on her contact page listed above.

MORE BOOKS BY FELICIA SLATTERY

Cash in On Communication:
Simple Tools for Entrepreneurs to Get
More Prospects, More Clients & More Cash Flow
through Effective Communication
(2010 – ParkHill Press – Out of Print –
New Edition coming in 2019)

21 Ways to Make Money Speaking
(2012 – Discover Books / ParkHill Press)
Available on Amazon.com and everywhere books are sold
Free Info: http://FeliciaSlattery.com/21ways

Kill The Elevator Speech:
Stop Selling, Start Connecting
(2014 - Sound Wisdom Press)
Available on Amazon.com and everywhere books are sold
Translated into Hindi
Free Info: http://KillTheElevatorSpeech.com

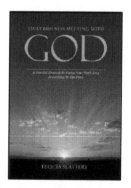

Daily Business Meeting with God:
A Special Journal to Focus Your Work Day
According to God's Plan
(2017 - ParkHill Press)
Available on Amazon.com and everywhere books are sold

Made in the USA
Columbia, SC
06 November 2018